THE
WHITEHALL PALACE PLAN
OF 1670

THE
WHITEHALL PALACE PLAN
OF 1670

By

SIMON THURLEY

London Topographical Society

Publication No. 153

1998

Publication no. 153 of the
London Topographical Society
3 Meadway Gate, London NW11

ISBN 0 902 087 401

PRINTED IN GREAT BRITAIN BY
W. S. MANEY & SON LTD, HUDSON ROAD, LEEDS

CONTENTS

ILLUSTRATIONS

ACKNOWLEDGEMENTS

This Publication has drawn on the skills and knowledge of a large number of people whom I wish to thank. Dr Andrew Barclay has given me a great deal of advice, including preparing biographical information for a dozen courtiers. He also read the manuscript in draft, making many helpful suggestions. Dr Sonya Wynne and Professor Robert Bucholz helped me identify several obscure courtiers. John Harris, Peter Barber and Sir Howard Colvin have given me advice on the interpretation of the manuscript plans. Dr Geoffrey Parnell advised me on the involvement of the Royal Ordnance. Dr Julia Merrit helped me with the wider Westminster context and David Jaques with the King's Gardener. Emily Cole and Anna Keay undertook most of the primary research in the Public Record Office. Clare Murphy from Historic Royal Palaces helped with the illustrations. Alasdair Hawkyard checked the text which was edited by Dr Ann Saunders and indexed by Dr Hana Sambrook. To all these people I am very grateful; without them this publication would never have seen the light of day. I must also acknowledge the help of the staff of the Museum of London — Mary Loxley, John Chase and Mireille Gallinou. The Museum has waived its reproduction fees for this volume.

SIMON THURLEY

Charles I

ABBREVIATIONS

BL	British Library
British Court	*The Present State of the British Court: or an Account of the Civil and Military Establishment of England* (London, 1720)
Cal. SP. Dom. (1856–1964)	*Calander of State Papers Domestic, 1547–1964*, 94 vols.
Colvin, *Dictionary*	H. M. Colvin, *A Biographical Dictionary of English Architects 1600–1840* (3rd edition, 1996)
DNB	*Dictionary of National Biography*, ed. Sir Leslie Stephen and Sir Sidney Lee, 66 vols. (1885–1901)
Evelyn	Evelyn, John, *Diary*, ed. E. S. de Beer, 6 vols, 1955.
HKW	*The History of the King's Works*, ed. H. M. Colvin, 6 vols. (1963–82)
Ordinances	*A Collection of Ordinances and Regulations for the Government of the Royal Household ... from King Edward III to King William and Queen Mary* (Society of Antiquaries, 1790)
Pepys	*The Diary of Samuel Pepys*, ed. Robert Latham and William Matthews, 11 vols. (1970–83)
ORH	J. C. Sainty and R. O. Bucholz, *Office Holders in Modern Britain*, Vol. XI, 'Officials of the Royal Household, 1660–1837', 2 parts (University of London Institute of Historical Research, 1997–8)
PRO	Public Records Office
SOL	*Survey of London*
WCA	Westminster City Archives

EDITOR'S NOTE

On the afternoon of 4 January 1698, in one of the apartments of Whitehall Palace, a maidservant spread linen to dry around a charcoal stove. The cloths ignited, a general conflagration ensued, and by the next morning a dozen people were dead, the servant girl among them, and the Palace itself was a smoking ruin. The King's and Queen's Apartments, the Royal Wardrobe, the Treasury, the Privy Office and the Office of the Secretary of State had all gone; Holbein's wall-painting of Henry VIII with his wife, Jane Seymour, and his parents, was ruined. The palace had covered some 23 acres; though the fire had been halted before it destroyed Scotland Yard, of the ceremonial buildings, Inigo Jones's Banqueting House was almost the sole survivor. John Evelyn entered in his Diary:

> Whitehall burnt utterly to the ground, nothing but the walls and ruines left

the Duc de Saint-Simon recorded sourly in his that the 'largest and ugliest palace' in Europe had been destroyed.

There was talk of rebuilding, of a new royal residence on a scale to rival Versailles, but there was neither the money nor the willpower to achieve it. The City of London had rebuilt itself for all commercial purposes in a mere three years after the Great Fire of 1666, but there was no such impetus to restore Whitehall. The site lay open and idle for a generation and more till in 1745–8, William Kent designed the Horse Guards building with a courtyard in front of it, towards Whitehall, and the Parade Ground behind, the work being completed after his death by John Vardy. Other buildings came to fill up the empty spaces and men forgot the enormous palace that had once sprawled out on either side of the thoroughfare.

The only record that remained was a ground plan, drawn up by Sir Christopher Wren's office in 1670 on the orders of Charles II. It was engraved by George Vertue in 1747 and is a plan pleasant enough to look at, but hard to comprehend and analyse. Vertue was working from a copy of the original survey, both of which are now lost. Other copies survive however, and we here publish, at full size, both Vertue's engraving and the Society of Antiquaries' seventeenth-century manuscript plan, which may have been one of the Office of Works' working drawings.

These plans are analysed in scholarly detail by Simon Thurley so that we can comprehend, for the first time in three centuries, what a vast and complex structure the Palace of Whitehall once was. His introduction includes a cast-list of those identified on the engraving, enabling us to begin to understand the intricacies of life at the Court of Charles II

Henrietta Maria

ANN SAUNDERS
Hon. Editor
London Topographical Society

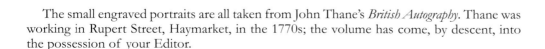

The small engraved portraits are all taken from John Thane's *British Autography*. Thane was working in Rupert Street, Haymarket, in the 1770s; the volume has come, by descent, into the possession of your Editor.

I. INTRODUCTION
WHITEHALL IN 1670

FROM 1530 when Henry VIII appropriated York Place from the fallen Cardinal Wolsey, till its destruction by fire in 1698, Whitehall Palace was the centre of royal life in England. As such it was also an artistic, political and social focus for the English nobility, and, indeed, the country at large. Sadly, for such an important building, the ferocity of the fire, and the subsequent expansion of Whitehall as government offices, have made it exceptionally hard to visualize this enormous and important building.

In attempting to understand Whitehall Palace the most important document we have is the survey datable to 1670, which is the subject of this publication. The survey shows an almost unintelligible mass of building. The Frenchman Sorbière, who saw Whitehall in 1665 considered the palace 'ill built, and nothing but a heap of houses erected at divers times, and of different Models, which they made contiguous in the best Manner they could for the Residence of the Court'. On hearing of its destruction, just over twenty years later, Saint-Simon recorded in his diary that the 'largest and ugliest' palace in Europe had burnt.

Whitehall Palace, in the 1670s, before Sir Christopher Wren began to rebuild it for James II and William III, owed its appearance to 140 years of pragmatic and piecemeal alteration by the Tudor and then the Stuart monarchs who, after Queen Elizabeth's death, began to extend the palace to accommodate a growing number of children, favourites and mistresses. Each had ambitions for a complete rebuilding, but all lacked the resources needed for a residence to equal the Escorial, the Louvre or any of the great European palaces. So, over a period of seventy years the palace grew organically from the inside out. New rooms were added forming links with old ones, courtyards were infilled, and old Tudor ranges were heightened. Meanwhile the awkward internal juxtapositions were cunningly disguised by a continual process of interior decoration and redecoration. Whilst the internal effect was judged a success, the exterior was an aesthetic disaster. This uncontrollable development rendered the principal seat of the English Crown completely architecturally incoherent.

Like Hampton Court, York Place, which became Whitehall Palace, had belonged to Cardinal Wolsey. He occupied it as Archbishop of York from 1514 and rapidly extended and improved the fifteenth-century house there which had been built by Archbishop Neville. By 1528 it was the largest and most modern house in Westminster and was only rivalled in London by the Archbishop of Canterbury's dwelling, Lambeth Palace, across the river.

Henry VIII

In 1512 the residential part of the Palace of Westminster, the ancient royal seat of English kings, had burnt down, and Henry VIII found himself the first king since before the Conquest without a residence in Westminster. For fifteen years the King was forced to borrow Lambeth Palace from Archbishop Warham and use a new palace at Bridewell in London by the River Fleet. In 1530, however, came a solution to his problems. The fall of Cardinal Wolsey provided the opportunity to appropriate York Place and transform it into a new principal residence.[1]

The scheme which Henry VIII executed at York Place in 1530–2 was the largest and most ambitious building programme ever completed by an English king. Not only did it set the form of the palace for the next century and a half, it laid out the bones of what is today modern Whitehall and St James's. In order to do this the King employed Thomas Cromwell to undertake a series of complex land transactions, resulting in the acquisition of the majority of the manor of Westminster — houses, shops, inns, fields, roads, streams and all.[2] The plan was drawn up over Christmas 1530 while Henry VIII and his mistress, Anne Boleyn, were at Greenwich and the first major campaign of building was rushed through for Anne's coronation in June 1533.

The scheme had four elements. First a riverside residential area centred on a long gallery which was to become known as the Privy Gallery. This was linked by a gatehouse, the so-called Holbein Gate, to a second area on the other side of King Street, the road which linked Westminster with Charing Cross. This area, the Park Side (later known as the Cockpit), was a recreation centre with four tennis courts, two bowling alleys and a cockpit. Beyond this to the west was the third element, a new park, today St James's Park, but originally the hunting park of Westminster Palace. In one corner of that was St James's palace, a former leper hospital bought from Eton College. This was intended as the home of the Prince of Wales, conveniently close to the King's own palace.

In its essentials this remained the layout of the palace until its destruction and Whitehall was rapidly to become Henry's favourite and most visited residence for the rest of his reign. The appearance of Whitehall on the King's death in 1547 was unusual. Its strong architectural forms were given distinction and visual coherence by a unique scheme of external decoration. The theme of the palace was black and white. The Holbein Gate was covered in a chequer pattern of black and white chalk and flints, as were the Cockpit and the battlements of the Chapel. The Great Hall was painted in black and white squares and the timber-framed parts were painted in grotesquework. This strong decorative theme, one of the few constants in the development of the palace, survived well into the seventeenth century — even Charles II laid out a black and white paved court-yard in his privy lodgings of 1666–7 (known as the Volery Lodgings).

Queen Elizabeth contributed little to the palace and on her death in 1603 it still retained the coherent appearance which Henry VIII's Master Masons and Carpenters had given it. The accession of James I, however, changed all this. James I, unlike Elizabeth, was married and had three children, all of whom needed accommodating at Whitehall. In 1603 King James started the process of conversion and extension which was to lead to the disintegration of Whitehall as an architectural entity. A tennis court was converted into a home for his daughter, Elizabeth, new rooms were squeezed in on the riverside for the Queen and lavish lodgings were made for his favourites and other courtiers. It is perhaps ironic that James I, whose architectural reputation rests on the construction of the Banqueting House at Whitehall, was the monarch who began the process of rendering the palace topographically incoherent.

The process of accretion which had begun in 1603 continued apace during the reign of Charles I. King Charles envisaged rebuilding the now hundred-year-old palace, along the lines of the Banqueting House. The Civil War ended these dreams, and instead the Banqueting House witnessed the spectacle of the King's execution. The palace then became the seat of the Council of State and later of Oliver Cromwell, as Lord Protector of England.

At the Restoration in 1660, Charles II inherited a palace which was still at core that of Henry VIII, now over a century old, and encrusted with later *ad hoc* additions. In the early 1660s, both the King and the aspiring John Webb produced a number of schemes for completely rebuilding the palace. However, by the late

Charles II envisaged him performing for his salary of £180 a year, but allegedly de la Fabvolière believed that Charles needed him more than he needed the King. The commission ended in disaster as, while in the lodgings of Prince Rupert, probably undertaking his survey work, he was 'abused' by some of the Prince's servants who then 'directed insufferable insults' against him. De la Fabvolière's reply must have been inflammatory — witnesses certainly thought so — and, in his own words 'four or five scoundrels of the Prince's Stable attacked me, dealt me several blows, and with my very own sword struck me on the head in two or three places ... covered in blood as I was ... I was kicked out of the door and onto the stairs'.[22] The engineer ended up first in the Porter's Lodge and then in the Porter's Prison in the Palace Gatehouse for causing an affray and drawing his sword at Court. On 5 March 1669, with both his commission and his career in England at an end, he wrote to Secretary of State Arlington from prison pleading to be released.[23]

As de la Fabvolière's replacement, Wren named Ralph Greatorex, who was instructed to survey and describe 'in vellom an Exact Ground plott of ye whole house of White hall, Cockpit & parts adjacent' for the sum of £60.[24] Greatorex (d. 1675) was a mathematical instrument maker and inventor and moved in the same scientific circle as Wren. He had previously been closely involved with the group of surveyors and instrument makers who mapped the remains of the City of London after the Great Fire. His name, and that of Jonas Moore the mathematician and surveyor, appear on the engraved version of Leake's plan of the ruined City.[25] But the reason for choosing him was almost certainly the fact that during 1668–9 Greatorex had been engaged by the Ordnance Office to undertake a large-scale survey of the Royal Arsenal at Woolwich for which he was paid in January 1670.[26] It must have been the satisfactory completion of this important commission, together with Wren's own knowledge of his work, that commended Greatorex for the task. Whitehall Palace, with its very dense and congested layout and complex property tenures, resembled much of the City of London and covered an area approximately the same acreage of that of the Arsenal. The work at Whitehall, presumably with a number of assistants, took nine months between February and October 1670. Greatorex's survey, a vellum master-copy presumably retained by the Office of Works, is now lost and so are his other surveys. Particularly interesting would have been the commission he received after the Whitehall work — a survey of the town and Castle of Windsor completed in 1672 which would have presumably been similar to the Whitehall survey.[27]

In attempting to visualize the Whitehall survey we have to rely on the surviving versions of the plan which were based on it and which were convincingly dated by the *Survey of London* to 1670.[28] All the new material gleaned for this publication confirms the accuracy of that dating and the reasons for it are not restated here. At least three plans were taken from the master survey, one now also lost. First, there was a plan formerly in the possession of the Duke of Portland, copied by George Vertue and published in 1747 (*Vertue's plan*), (Plan A), then there is a plan in the British Museum Crace drawings (*the Crace plan*), (Plan B) and finally one in the Society of Antiquaries (*the Antiquaries' plan*), (Plan C). It is necessary to examine the evidence contained within each of these in some detail.[29]

First, the two manuscript plans. The Crace plan (BL, Crace Plans XI, 65) (Plan B) is in pen and wash and measures 625 mm by 810 mm, and has been cut into two and pasted onto thin card. It forms part of the collection amassed between 1829 and 1859 by the interior decorator, Frederick Crace (1779–1859), and sold to the British Museum by his family in 1880 for £3,000. It is not known how Crace came to own the plan, although there are several possibilities. One is that Frederick Crace may have inherited the plan, and others, from his father John who held the appointment of Painter to the Board of Works and thus would have had access to Works plans.[30] Another is that the plan was, in fact, acquired by his son J. G. Crace who, it appears, augmented his father's collection of plans between 1859 and 1880. J. G. Crace could have come into contact with the Whitehall drawing, for instance, whilst working on the Palace of Westminster with Pugin after 1844. However the single most likely way that the plan entered the Crace collection was through Frederick Crace himself. Frederick had had a long-standing fascination with the topography of London. He collected views, maps and plans of London for their topographical and factual content, and on his death had amassed 5,000 prints and drawings. It is likely that the Whitehall plan was one of these.[31]

The Antiquaries' plan (Society of Antiquaries MS 196 G) (Plan C) is slightly smaller than the Crace plan, measuring 530 mm by 750 mm. It too has been backed, but with linen, and unlike the Crace plan is uncut. The provenance of this plan is far less certain but it is just possible that there is a connection with George Vertue. He could either have encouraged the Antiquaries to acquire the plan or the Antiquaries could have acquired it having recognized its importance through his copy of the plan which he engraved (see below).

The two plans are very similar. Both cover only part of the palace, but neither is a fragment. Both have a carefully drawn black line, ruled 3 mm from the edge of the paper, leaving an unmarked white margin proving them both to be their original size. The Crace plan shows slightly more than the Antiquaries' plan on the north, south and west sides but otherwise the plans are identical in content. A number of very minor discrepancies can be identified, but these are clearly errors. Two examples can be cited to illustrate this point:

1. The Antiquaries' plan has an area of wash to the east of the chapel to the south of the room labelled the 'outward vestry'. In the Crace version this area of wash is defined by walls.

2. At the west end of the privy gallery the Crace plan shows a staircase and a small room in the corner marked 'O'. The Antiquaries' plan shows neither, but is clearly unfinished with a wash line which stands alone from the pen line.

Both these discrepancies are errors consistent with the work of a copyist working from a third, lost plan. Neither demonstrates that the plans are materially different. In all other respects, including the colour-coding, the plans match in matters of minute detail. A particularly telling similarity is the pencilled statues in the centre of each plot in the Privy Garden. This leads to the likelihood that the plans emerged from the same office and were perhaps both copies of a lost original. Sadly, due to the fact that both plans have been subsequently backed, it has not been possible to determine whether either had been pricked for transfer. However, on the basis of the handwriting of some of the annotations, it can be conclusively demonstrated that the plans were annotated by the same hand and were therefore probably produced by the same office in a similar time scale.

Both plans have annotations in a number of different hands; however, one of these is of a seventeenth-century type which uses the characteristic reversed e. Annotations such as 'The Guard House', 'Queens Bake House' and 'Foot Guard House' not only use the reverse e but are in the same hand — 'Queens Bake House' is even written sideways on both plans. Many of the upper case annotations are also identical, particularly 'THE BANQVETING HOUSE'. The match of handwriting, together with the evidence presented above for a common source, leads to the conclusion that the two plans were both copies of an original produced by the same office at a similar period. The key question is when they were produced. The evidence suggests very strongly that the plans were copies made from the Greatorex survey within a short time after its completion. There are a number of reasons for believing this.

1. The first and most compelling is that the production of such a plan, particularly with multi-coloured washes, was a laborious, time-consuming and expensive process. The buildings which are shown on the plan only existed in the form depicted for a short time after 1670 as by 1682 the King had effected a major rebuilding which had altered the whole of the area between the Privy Gallery and the Volery Lodgings. After 1682, and possibly earlier, there would have been no point in reproducing this plan to such a high standard, since the building it showed no longer existed.

2. In addition to this, as has already been observed, many of the annotations are in a hand which exhibits the seventeenth-century characteristic of a reversed e. This rarely appears after about 1700 and therefore would suggest a seventeenth-century date.[32] In addition the terminology and spelling of the annotations also point to a seventeenth-century date. The use of the words 'ground-platt' on the Antiquaries' plan and the spelling of words like 'cole' and 'chappell' are seventeenth-century rather than mid-eighteenth-century or later. This, of course, does not preclude the possibility that the plans are later copies which faithfully reproduced earlier conventions.

3. Although watermarks are a notoriously difficult way of dating works on paper, and do not offer conclusive evidence in this case, it is important to note that the evidence from a watermark on the Antiquaries' plan does not preclude a date of 1670. It has a watermark, 'I Villedary' which, although it is unlikely to be later than the late eighteenth century, is not incompatible with the period 1670–80.[33]

4. In terms of drawing technique both plans exhibit seventeenth-century tendencies, which alone cannot prove a date of 1670, but together with the evidence above, contribute towards the overall picture. Both plans show the statues in the Privy Garden in elevation with a shadow in dark wash. The scale is of a seventeenth-century type and the use of water-colour washes, particularly to show the river on the Crace plan, exhibits the seventeenth-century tension between an architectural plan and topographical view.[34]

5. Finally the evidence presented by the additional annotations should be considered. In addition to the annotations, which are here considered to be contemporary, there are a number in different hands. These include all the annotations that make up the key along the bottom of the Antiquaries' plan (but not the scale) and a number of annotations on the Antiquaries' plan itself. 'Lord newports', 'Privy Garden' and 'Private Wine Cellar' fall into this category. On the Crace plan there is the title 'Plan of the Palace of White Hall' and 'This Plan taken about the latter end of King Charles IIds reign or about 1680', both of which are in a different hand.

There are a number of points that can be made about these additional annotations which help the issue of dating. Several can be shown to have been added soon after 1670. For instance the passage from the Court Gate to the Guard Chamber is called the 'new' covered passage on an annotation on the Crace plan. This passage was completed in July 1669. The Crace plan has a later addition in the room between those marked 21 and 24. Here a staircase has been inserted which does not show on the Antiquaries' plan but is on Vertue's engraved version. The addition of such a minor feature would again suggest contemporary knowledge or concern.

The Antiquaries' plan too has annotations which suggest immediate contemporary knowledge. Most telling is the additional annotation 'D Lauderdales Kitchen' and on the key 'Lord Lauderdale'. Lauderdale was created a Duke in 1672 and he left Whitehall in 1675 when his lodgings passed into the hands of the 2nd Earl of Rochester. The room identified as his kitchen can be shown, from other contemporary sources, to have been

Fig. 2. *London &c. Actually survey'd and a Prospect of London and Westminster.* By William Morgan 1682.

In the foreground are the King's Volery lodgings on the left, the Queen's lodgings in the centre, and the Privy Kitchen on the waterfront at the right. In the background is the Great Tennis Court (converted for Monmouth), the Banqueting House, and the Great Hall and Chapel.

so. His title 'Lord lauderdale' on the Antiquaries' plan does not match his earlier title 'earl of Lauderdale' on Vertue's engraved version. This annotation therefore suggests the contemporary use of the plan in the years 1672–5.

The lettering and numbering on the plans show that, in the versions which have come down to us, the purpose of the plan was to illustrate the location and extent of various lodgings granted to people associated with the King and his Court. In other words the plan had a functional and not an architectural purpose. The colour-coding and sepia washes are therefore also likely to have represented functional distinctions rather than architectural ones. A brief examination of the evidence would suggest that this is true. First let us consider the blue and red colour-coding of the walls. The first possibility is that the colours of the walls represent different materials, either brick, stone or timber-framing. This can not be the case as the Banqueting House (stone), the Great Hall (brick), and the Tiltyard Gallery (timber-framed) are all shown as blue. The second is that one colour represents new buildings, the other old ones. This must also be rejected as both the King's Volery Lodgings of 1666 and the Chapel of 1528 are blue. A third possibility is that while one colour signified walls that were to be demolished, the other represented walls which were to be retained. This theory relates to no known scheme, and the distribution of the colouring makes this very unlikely. Finally, it could be said that the blue walls were outer walls and the red, inner. This, however, would not hold true of Scotland Yard. Other options could be considered but none accords with an architectural explanation of the colour-coding.

In considering the significance of the wash, the same conclusions apply. The simplest explanation would be that the areas of wash either represented covered or open areas, making a distinction between buildings and courtyards. However this can be dismissed as, for instance, the Volery Garden (an open area) is shaded whilst the lodgings of the Pages of the Backstairs (number 7) are not; a large part of the Duke of Albermarle's yard is shaded whilst the gallery outside the Comptrollers (y) and Sir John Trevor's lodging (27) is not. Like the colour-coding, the areas of sepia cannot be shown to be linked to architectural distinctions.

Having rejected several traditional interpretations of colour-coding, what can be deducted from its usage? It has already been noted that the plans are not fragments of a larger one but were specifically drawn to that size. An examination of the distribution of the blue walls suggests that the size of the plan was determined by their location. The northernmost point of both plans is defined by the

Restoration lack sufficient detail to chronicle the development of this subsidiary accommodation, but enough information exists to facilitate a good understanding of what, in broad terms, had taken place by the end of Charles I's reign. In November 1637 George Gerrard wrote that 'the court is now filled with families of every mean courtier',[44] an observation which indicates the increase in number of courtier lodgings on the eve of the Civil War. Greater substance to this is given by the inventory of royal pictures compiled for Charles I by Abraham van der Doort from 1637. Van der Doort lists seven large courtier lodgings leading off the Matted Gallery[45] which by then served as a spine leading to lodgings on its east side. After the Restoration Charles II was to develop the Matted Gallery further as the most prestigious location for lodgings in the palace. But during the reign of Charles I lodgings were built in other parts of the palace too. One of the very few references in the account rolls for such work is for building two rooms for the Vice-Chamberlain, Sir Robert Killigrew, who had rooms set up for him in the riverside gallery running from the Privy Bridge to the Prince's Lodgings.[46]

Catharine of Braganza, Charles II's Queen

During the Republic Whitehall had been used as a government office block housing parliamentary committees and those who served on them, and by the Restoration the palace was in a poor state. As we have seen above, Charles II's objective in 1660 had been to rebuild the palace and recreate the magnificence of his father's court. At first sight this was a perfectly realizable ambition as the form and running of the royal household was almost completely the King's own affair, as was how he spent money on it. However, very soon after his coronation Charles II was to realize that his ambition could not be fulfilled.

Charles II's household, like that of his predecessors, was divided into three great departments, that of the Lord Chamberlain, the Lord Steward and the Master of the Horse. The Lord Chamberlain's department was the largest, responsible for the running of the above stairs functions of the court and staffed, at its peak, by almost 900 officers. At its head was the Lord Chamberlain, in 1670 the Earl of Manchester. The department was divided into a number of sub-departments, the most powerful of which was the semi-autonomous Bedchamber headed by a peer and staffed by between twenty and forty Gentlemen, Grooms and Pages. It was the duty of the Bedchamber to provide personal services to the King. The Lord Steward's department was smaller and shrank during the reign from about 350 staff to 150 staff. The department was headed by the Lord Steward who delegated the running of the department to the Board of the Green Cloth, a committee of great officers and senior clerks. They were responsible for all the downstairs functions of the court. The third great department was that of the Master of the Horse with a staff of around 170 officials. It was their duty to provide for the needs of transport and equine recreation.[47]

In 1660, amidst a scramble for rewards, Charles II had the task of appointing all the key post holders to these departments. Soon there were over 300 salaried officials below stairs and the Household Kitchen was brought back into operation so that royal servants could be fed at the King's table as before the Civil War. These free meals, known as diets, were the principal form of remuneration for many household staff, but the more important were also rewarded with livery (clothing, or money in lieu of it), plate or domestic supplies such as light or fuel. Many were also rewarded with a grant of a lodging at one or more of the palaces. The package granted to servants could thus be very lucrative. For example Sir Gilbert Talbot, the Master of the Jewel House, estimated that his place was worth at least £1,000 a year to him. This included a diet worth £700, rights

Fig. 5.   *Arrival of Charles II at Whitehall in 1660 (c. 1660).* Attributed to Issac Fuller. Fotomans Index.

In the background to the right, is the long range of offices built by Queen Elizabeth which formed an independent part of the accommodation available to courtiers in Scotland Yard.

to ambassadorial gifts worth £200 and poundage on New Year's gifts worth £150. In addition he had lodgings at Whitehall as well as rooms at the Tower of London.[48]

By the autumn of 1662 there were 1,357 sworn and paid servants in the household. But this scale of operation soon proved to be insupportable. It was almost impossible to control a system of diets economically, and by December 1662, with spiralling costs and mounting debts, there were tough cutbacks and a reduction of below stairs servants to about 220. Even this draconian measure, greeted with loud protests from officials, was not enough. In August 1663 almost all the remaining diets in the Lord Steward's department were abolished and staff numbers reduced to 147. A new establishment issued in 1664 confirmed these arrangements. This was a fundamental break in the history of the royal household; for the first time only a small number of body servants would receive free meals, and everyone else had to feed themselves at mealtimes as best they could.[49]

Whilst the number of members of the King's household decreased, the size of the King's family increased. This phenomenon created an enormous official and unofficial royal family, all of whom had their households, servants and lodgings at Whitehall. The most important of these was King's brother, James, Duke of York (later James II) and his wives, first Anne Hyde, Duchess of York until her death in March 1671, and then Mary of Modena, the future Queen whom he married in November 1673. In addition, other significant residents included the King's cousin Prince Rupert until his death in 1682, and most importantly a large number of mistresses and their children. James Scott, the Duke of Monmouth and Buccleuch, born in the Hague by Lucy Walters, Charles's mistress at the time of his exile; Barbara Palmer, Countess Castlemaine and subsequently Duchess of Cleveland, who bore him a child a year between 1661 and 1665; Nell Gwynne who bore him two sons; Louise Renée de Kerouaille, subsequently

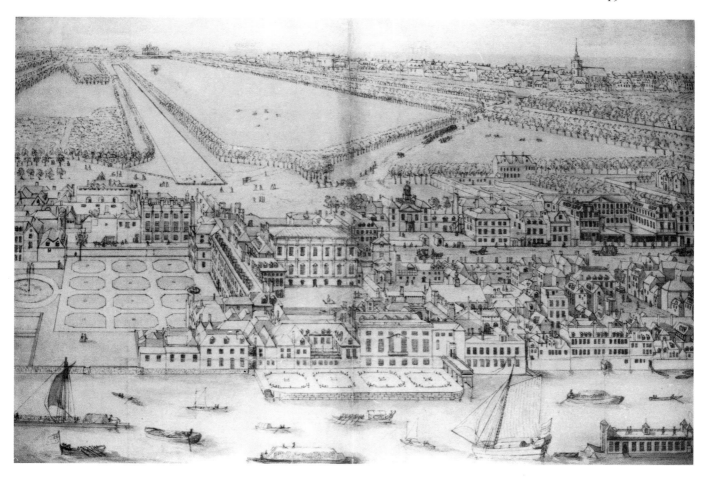

the Duchess of Portsmouth, whose son was made Duke of Richmond; and Catherine Pegge, the mistress of his Spanish exile, who bore him a son, popularly known as Don Carlos. These facts are the important backdrop to the plan and lodgings list of 1670, made up only eight years after the radical changes to the size of the household and in the early years of the expansion of the King's family.

On 4 July 1659 an order was issued to clear Whitehall within six days of all those who were lodging there unless given specific permission to remain.[50] This was a prelude to the Restoration when entirely new warrants would be issued for lodgings at Whitehall. Within weeks of the King's return, warrants began to be issued by the Lord Chamberlain authorizing lodgings to be given over to specific courtiers. Amongst the earliest warrants are those to one Widow Spittlehouse, Mr King and Mr Firbank, who was granted two rooms and a closet.[51] The fact that there is only an incomplete record of these grants suggests that much of the early distribution of lodgings at Whitehall was undertaken verbally by the King and his principal officers. By January 1661 this informal process had caused so much confusion and contradiction that the Under Housekeeper, George Vaux, received the following order: 'Whereas I am informed that diverse persons have possessed themselves of lodgings in his magesties pallace of Whitehall without my order having right to noe lodgings there. These are therefore to will and require you forthwith to take an expresse of all the lodgings in whitehall and who are in them and by what right they are soe possessed'.[52] The record produced by Vaux does not survive, but after early 1661 the Lord Chamberlain's warrant

Fig. 6. *Bird's eye view of White-hall Palace* (*c.* 1695–7). By Leonard Knyff. Pen and ink drawing, 31 x 21¾ inches. Reproduced by permission of Westminster City Archives.

Drawn after the fire of 1691 when the Palace was being rebuilt. The view, however, shows Scotland Yard and the Cockpit much as they were in 1670.

books give the impression of a more ordered and controlled process for the granting of lodgings.

The Lord Chamberlain and the Vice Chamberlain distributed lodgings both above and below stairs by warrant to the Gentlemen Ushers' Daily Waiters who had the task of delivering them to the occupants.[53] Soon after the completion of the 1670 plan in March 1671/2 the Gentlemen Ushers were ordered to 'take an exact survey of all the lodgings within the palace of Whitehall and the name of the occupants entered in a book'.[54] The annotation on the Antiquaries' plan identifying the Duke of Lauderdale's kitchen (see above) may be a result of this survey. The 1670 plan only shows the lodgings on the ground floor of the palace which represented about two-thirds of the space available for courtiers and officers. The survey taken of the lodgings at Whitehall in 1689 listed 1,161 rooms, 55 closets, 75 garrets, 26 cellars, 13 kitchens and two shops. In addition there were at least 143 rooms, 27 closets, three cellars and five kitchens belonging to the Queen's servants.[55] Therefore, without taking into account the rooms for the King and Queen themselves, Whitehall had over 1,500 rooms set aside for lodging.

In addition to their role as distributors of lodgings, the Gentlemen Ushers' Daily Waiters were responsible for policing the system. When a dispute arose, they would be ordered to investigate. In May 1661 Sir John Ayton (Gentleman Usher 1660–72) investigated the lodging rights of the Sewers of the Chamber whose lodging had been appropriated by the Porters.[56] This policing role was often shared with the Housekeeper and Under Housekeeper. We have already seen that the survey of lodgings in 1661 was undertaken by George Vaux, but after the appointment of George Kirke as Keeper of the Palace in February 1664, he assumed responsibility for many of the practical aspects of enforcement.[57]

An area of particular concern for the Keeper and Ushers was fire. As early as the autumn of 1662 all residents were ordered to 'provide themselves with leather buckets ... and to be ready in case of accident'.[58] But the Great Fire of London in September 1666 gave rise to even greater concern for Whitehall, the safety of which had barely been threatened, but which would have been rapidly consumed if the fire had caught it. Just before the Fire, George Kirke had been ordered to sweep all the chimneys, but in December, with the City in ruins, Sir John Ayton was tasked to survey all the lodgings in the palace to establish the number of chimneys, and therefore the number of buckets that needed to be provided for fire prevention.[59]

It is difficult either from household regulations, or from the Lord Chamberlain's warrants, to determine with any certainty the rules for the distribution of lodgings at Whitehall. The explanation is probably because there were none. The Gazetteer below shows that while some people had lodgings by right, many had them through the King's personal favour, and it is very difficult to be dogmatic about why people had lodging rights. Even so, a number of generalizations can be made. There were certainly some groups of people who were awarded lodgings as part of their remuneration. These fell into two groups: those who had the use of a room or rooms whilst they were on duty, and those who were granted a permanent lodging. The small group of body servants who had diets were given a lodging in which to eat their meals. For example two rooms occupied by the Porters in Scotland Yard were returned to the Sewers of the Chamber because the 'roomes are necessary for a place to eate their dyett in'.[60] A number of other groups had similar lodgings including the Gentlemen and unauthorized building works which might jeopardize either the lodging itself or its neighbour, financial claims against the Crown, obstruction of royal architectural plans, failure to maintain set building standards and many more. These issues had concerned the monarchy since Tudor times and became more pressing after 1660 due to the expansion in courtier lodgings.

As early as 1663 an order had been given that 'no alterations or repairs in our houses of Whitehall ... which shall exceed ye summe of £40 within ye space of one year ... without directions and orders from ye officers of ye works ... and they in any considerable repaires & new buildings not without special warrant from the Lord Treasurer' to be obtained by directions of the Lord Chamberlain.[72] But the order had little effect, mainly because the Office of Works would not abide by it. In July 1667 an anonymous critique of the Office of Works was submitted to the Treasury. It came at a time when strict financial limits were being set on its activities (and those of most other departments) and recommended a number of changes to eliminate waste and corruption. One of the observations was that officials of the Works tended to 'gain friends [at court] by doing works for them'.[73] This practice was widespread and Pepys records the discomfort felt by Hugh May when he had to refuse friends and acquantances 'what they desire to [do to] their lodgings'. Probably as a result of this document an order was issued the same month stating that 'no alteracons [shall be made] except for the King and Queen and Dukes apartments, other than to keep wind and water tight. What else be at the partyes charge'.[74] This was a much stricter regime and one that was presumably reinforced by the colour-coded version of the 1670 plan issued three years later. These controls appear to have been more effective and are reflected in the Lord Chamberlain's Warrant Books. For instance on 3 July 1667 a warrant was issued for Wren to repair the lodgings of the Maids of Honour and the Queen's starcher Mrs Nunn,[75] and another was issued by Lord Arlington for the repair of a little room in the Greencloth Yard for the use of Mrs Jones, necessary woman to the Queen, 'but soe that it be not higher than the roome adjoyning lately repaired, that it may not offend mr. vice chamberlayne'.[76] Yet only a small proportion of repair and building work on non-royal lodgings at Whitehall was undertaken by the Office of Works. The 1670 plan illustrates this graphically by the relatively small area of blue walling. By far the greatest amount of development and repair was funded and organized by the occupants of the lodgings, rich or poor. Lord Mandeville, for instance, was granted permission to build over the gallery 'towards St James's Park' with 'his owne workemen' and at his own cost.[77] Thomas Povey, the Duke of York's Treasurer, was given leave to construct a new building for himself with a new entrance onto the Stone Gallery, making his lodgings larger and grander, with their own front door.[78]

The King soon found that the orders of 1667, which did little to regulate courtier building, brought their own problems as unregulated courtier develop-ment meant that the 'ye [King's] houses are weakened and ye repaires become more chargable, the freedome of aire is less & ye spring & conduits of water exhausted' and so in 1674 new regulations were issued to Wren. These decreed that 'no new or additional building bee for ye future made or erected or any great or considerable alterations made' without permission from the Treasury. But even with permission courtier building activity could lead to serious disputes as the example of the Earl of Dorset's lodgings shows. In September 1681 the Earl of Dorset obtained permission to build another storey onto his lodging in the Privy Garden. This lodging, which dated from the reign of Charles I, had been latterly occupied by Sir Robert Murray and is shown on the 1670 plan. Permis-

Fig. 8. *The Lord Mayor's Water Procession on the Thames* (1683). Anonymous oil painting. Reproduced by gracious permission of Her Majesty The Queen.

Painted only a few years after 1670, this view shows the Duke of York's lodgings above the Prince's Lodgings in the centre.

sion was granted to extend on the condition that the new work would not be prejudicial to the Privy Gallery. As far as we know it was not. However it was prejudicial to the view of another near neighbour, the Duchess of Cleveland, who had rooms in and around the Holbein Gate. In December 1681 an order was issued 'to stop the building that is in the privy garden at the Earle of Dorsetts Lodgings from going any further, and that you suffer none of the lights of the Dutchesse of Clevelande lodgings to bee stopped up or any wayes changed'.[79] Building seems to have stopped and the plans were changed. Others who built without permission were treated more harshly. Hugh May was instructed to remove certain 'shedds of boards' that had been erected in the passage to the Queen's Lord Chamberlain's lodgings in May 1666.[80]

Sometimes permission was given for occupants to organize and pay for the building (or rebuilding) of their own lodgings or offices and re-charge the cost to the King. This type of private enterprise construction presumably relieved the pressure on the Office of Works. The Treasury, for instance, reimbursed James Gibbons, Clerk of the Robes and Wardrobes, £300 which he had laid out in building lodgings for his office, and Henry Sidney was paid an allowance of £800 by the King from his Secret Service account to reimburse him for work on his lodgings at Whitehall.[81]

Unreimbursed expenditure on lodgings at Whitehall gave occupants considerable rights over their buildings. Indeed, as the reign advanced, lodgings, especially in Scotland Yard and on the Park Side, were held under lease. In September 1673 the King gave notice to Sir Christopher Wren that permission had been granted to Thomas Wyndham, one of the Grooms of the King's Bedchamber, to build a house, at his own cost, in Greencloth Yard (near N and M) near Sir Alexander Frazier.[82] In December 1678 Wyndham was granted a thirty-one-year lease on his house.[83] Ten years later Patrick Lamb, the Sergeant of the Pastry, was

Notes

[1] Simon Thurley, 'Whitehall Palace and Westminster 1400–1600: A Royal Seat in Transition', David Gaimster and Paul Stamper (eds.), *The Age of Transition. The Archaeology of English Culture 1400–1600* (Society for Medieval Archaeology Monograph 15, 1997), pp. 93–104.

[2] Gervase Rosser and Simon Thurley, 'Whitehall Palace and King Street Westminster: The Urban Cost of Princely Magnificence', *London Topographical Record*, vol. XXVI (1990), pp. 57–77.

[3] S. Thurley, 'A Country Seat fit for a King: Charles II, Greenwich and Winchester 1660–1685', E. Cruikshanks (ed.), *The Stuart Court* (forthcoming).

[4] L. R. Shelby explores this and the subject of early Tudor plan drawing in L. R. Shelby, *John Rogers, Tudor Military Engineer* (Oxford, 1967), pp. 145–57.

[5] PRO Works 38/770; Hatfield House CPM II.20; BL Lansdowne Roll 18; *HKW*, vol. IV, pp. 151–3.

[6] Mark Girouard, 'The Smythson Collection of the Royal Institute of British Architects', *Architectural History*, vol. 5, (1962), pp. 72, 146.

[7] Kevin Sharpe, 'The Image of Virtue: the Court and Household of Charles I, 1625–1642', D.Starkey (ed.), *The English Court* (London, 1987), pp. 229–30.

[8] *Wren Society*, vol. VII, p. 234.

[9] E. S. de Beer, 'Whitehall Palace: Inigo Jones and Wren', *Notes and Queries*, 30 December 1939, pp. 471–3.

[10] The definitve discussion of these drawings and the other two schemes covered by this section is in M. Whinney, 'John Webb's Drawings for Whitehall Palace', *Walpole Society*, vol. 31 (1946), pp. 45–107. Dr Whinney's lettering of the schemes is followed here as in all publications subsequent to her article. An earlier analysis of the drawings which is important in the historiography of Whitehall is by J. A. Gotch, 'The Original Drawings for the Palace of Whitehall', *Architectural Review*, XXXI (1912), pp. 333–64. J. Bold in *John Webb* (Oxford, 1989), pp. 107–25 adds little new. J. Summerson, *Inigo Jones* (Harmondsworth, 1966), pp. 127–34, discusses Inigo Jones's part in the 'P' scheme.

[11] E. S. de Beer, *op. cit.*, pp. 471–2.

[12] PRO Work 5/1, fo. 155ᵛ.

[13] *Wren Society*, vol. XVIII, pp. 155–6.

[14] PRO Work 5/1, fo. 83.

[15] S. Thurley, 'A Country Seat fit for a King', *op. cit.*

[16] *The Diary of John Evelyn*, vol. III, p. 386; PRO Work 5/10, fo. 116.

[17] Kerry Downes, 'Wren and Whitehall in 1664', *The Burlington Magazine*, 113 (1971), pp. 89–92; S. Wren, *Parentalia, or Memoirs of the Family of the Wrens* (London, 1750), p. 334.

[18] PRO 31/14/212, fo. 9ᵛ (*Cal. SP. Ven., 1664–6*, p. 55).

[19] *Cal. SP. Dom., 1668–9*, pp. 227, 615; E. S. de Beer, *op. cit.*, p. 472.

[20] PRO LC5/12, p. 232.

[21] PRO SP29/173, p. 102.

[22] PRO SP29/112, p. 9.

[23] PRO SP29/267, p. 107A.

[24] PRO Work 5/15, fo. 100.

[25] Frances Willmoth, *Sir Jonas Moore, Practical Mathematics and Restoration Science* (Woodbridge, 1993), p. 137.

[26] PRO WO51/11, p. 42. Dr Geoffrey Parnell drew this to my attention.

[27] *Dictionary of Land Surveyors and Local Mapmakers of Great Britain and Ireland 1530–1850*, 2 vols. (British Library, 1997).

[28] By the *SOL*, vol. XIII, pp. 41–3. Work on Whitehall for this publication, and printed in the Gazetteer, has confirmed that the dating given in 1930 is correct.

[29] The first analysis of these plans can be found in *SOL*, vol. XIII, pp. 41–4; also see *HKW*, vol. V, pp. 264–5.

[30] Megan Aldrich (ed.), *The Craces: Royal Decorators 1768–1899* (Brighton, 1990), p. 9.

[31] *Ibid.*, pp. 31–2. Peter Barber, who has recently rewritten the catalogue of the Crace Collection, was kind enough to communicate unpublished information to me.

[32] The plan could, however, have been annotated by someone with old-fashioned handwriting working in the early eighteenth century.

[33] Edward Heawood, *Monumenta Chartae Papyracae I. Watermarks of the Seventeenth and Eighteenth Century* (Paper Publications Society, 1940), pl. 248 (nos. 1809, 1810, p. 105).

[34] Iolo Williams, *Early English Watercolours and some Cognate Drawings by Artists born not later than 1785* (London, 1952), pp. 4–12.

[35] *HKW*, vol. v, p. 436. Sir Howard Colvin pointed this out to me.

[36] Geoffrey Parnell, *London Topographical Society*, Publication No. 129 (1983), pp. 72–9 'Fine Seventeenth-Century Plans of the Tower of London'.

[37] *Walpole Society*, vol. 18 (1929–30), 'Vertue Note Books, Vol. I', p. 8.

[38] *Walpole Society*, vol. 26 (1937–8), 'Vertue Note Books, Vol. V', pp. 70–1; vol. 18 (1929–30), 'Vertue Note Books, Vol. I', p. 19.

[39] PRO LR 9/107.

[40] *Dictionary of Land Surveyors, op. cit.*

[41] R. V. Tooley, *Tooley's Dictionary of Mapmakers* (Tring, 1979), p. 213. Buckinghamshire Record Office D/RA/3/71/T. Todd Longstaffe-Gowan provided me with this reference.

[42] S. Thurley, 'English Royal Palaces 1450–1550', unpublished Ph.D. thesis (London, 1990), Appendix II.

[43] BL Egerton MS 2026, fo. 23.

[44] *The Earl of Strafford's Letters and Dispatches*, ed. W. Knowler, 2 vols. (London, 1739), vol. II, p. 129.

[45] BL Harl. MS 4718; for the contents of the gallery see Arthur MacGregor (ed.), *The Late King's Goods* (London and Oxford, 1989); O. Millar (ed. with an Introduction), 'The Inventories and Valuations of the King's Goods 1649–1651', *Walpole Society*, vol. 43 (1970–2).

[46] PRO E351/3265.

[47] A very useful summary of this is in *ORH*, pp. liii-lx.

[48] *ORH*, p. xl.

[49] Andrew Barclay, 'The Impact of King James II on the Departments of the Royal Household', unpublished Ph.D. thesis, University of Cambridge, 1993, pp. 69–77; A. Barclay, 'Charles II's failed restoration: administrative reform belowstairs, 1660–1664', E. Cruikshanks (ed.), *The Stuart Court* (forthcoming).

[50] PRO SP25/79, fo. 40.

[51] PRO SP25/79, p. 191; SP25/85, pp. 212–17.

[52] PRO LC5/137, p. 320.

[53] *Ordinances*, p. 369.

[54] PRO LC5/140, p. 67.

[55] BL Lansdowne MS 736, fo. 18^r.

[56] PRO LC5/137, p. 310.

[57] PRO SP38/22, fo. 20. The entry for this in *Cal. SP. Dom., 1663–4*, p. 45 is incorrect in its dating, the document is dated February 1664.

[58] PRO SP29/66, p. 10.

[59] PRO LC5/138, pp. 367, 369.

[60] PRO LC5/137, p. 310.

[61] PRO LC5/138, p. 430.

[62] *HKW*, vol. v, pp. 443–51.

[63] PRO LC5/139, p. 368. For Fox see below.

[64] BL Harl. MS 1843, item 12.

[65] PRO LC5/145, p. 102.

[66] *SOL*, vol. xiv, pp. 51–2; BL Add. MS 28,053, fos. 282–3.

[67] J. Y. Ackerman (ed.), 'Moneys Received and Paid for Secret Services of Charles II and James II', *Camden Society* (1851), pp. 9, 13, 16, 20, 22, 29.

[68] *Ibid.*, p. 115.

[69] *Ibid.*, p. 83.

[70] PRO LC5/138, p. 281.

[71] PRO LC5/139, p. 368.

[72] PRO SP29/88, p. 1^v.

[73] *HKW*, vol. v, pp. 11–15, 23–4.

[74] PRO T29/1.

[75] PRO LC5/138, p. 347.

[76] PRO SP29/372, p. 21 (July 1675).

[77] PRO LC5/138, p. 359.

[78] PRO LC5/138, p. 424.

[79] PRO LC5/144, p. 124.

[80] PRO LC5/138, p. 359.

[81] PRO SP44/71, p. 341; J. Y. Ackerman, *op. cit.*, pp. 121–2.

[82] PRO LC5/140, p. 329; *SOL*, vol. XVI, p. 186.

[83] *SOL*, vol. XVI, p. 186.

[84] PRO LC5/145, p. 156; *SOL*, vol. XVI, p. 165.

[85] J. Y. Ackerman, *op. cit.*, p. 52.

[86] PRO SP29/293, p. 56.

[87] PRO SP44/338, p. 347.

[88] PRO LS 13/172, p. 27.

[89] PRO LS 13/174, p. 141.

[90] PRO LC5/148, p. 112.

[91] *Ordinances*, p. 369; see the Lord Chamberlain's Warrant books which are complete for Charles II reign: PRO LC5/60-LC5/69.

[92] PRO Work 5/61, fos. 29, 313; LC5/60, p. 189.

[93] Colvin, *Dictionary*, pp. 70–100.

[94] WCA MS H450.

[95] BL Add. MS 28,053, fo. 283.

[96] PRO SP29/395, p. 24.

King William and Queen Mary

Mr Chase — John Chase (d. 1690)
Apothecary to the King, 1660–85

John Chase succeeded his father, Stephen, as Apothecary to Charles I and at the Restoration secured the reversion of the post for his son James. As Royal Apothecary Chase's duties ranged from providing the King's bath salts to powders for keeping the King's clothes smelling sweet. In 1667 Chase complained about the level of his remuneration and claimed that Charles II owed him £6,000.[35]

His lodging (number 30) was in Little Scotland Yard, appropriately sited beside that of the Doctor of the Household, Thomas Waldron (q.v.) and the Groom Porter, Thomas Offley (q.v.). A warrant was issued on 14 January 1663–4 to pay £208 'out of the treasure of the chamber ... to john Chase esq. ... who hath beene at great charges in buildinge of the howse and office belonginge to his place within his Magesties Pallace of Whitehall'.[36] This suggests that the two rooms and what appears to have been a yard which the 1670 plan shows, were built by him in the early years of the reign. Unfortunately we have no details of the lodging and the Works accounts only mention it once.

Yet it is known that he was provided, 'as was customary' by the Great Wardrobe, with two great 'collars' or cupboards with partitions and drawers, with pots and glasses and 'leather for coverings'. He was also given two travelling chests for transporting his potions on progress.[37] In September 1661 Chase was visited in his Whitehall dispensary by Pepys and his friend John Battersby, an apothecary from Fenchurch Street, 'and there drank a bottle or two of wine'.[38]

In addition to his lodging at Whitehall, Chase had a chemist's shop in Henrietta Street, Covent Garden, from 1660.[39]

Mr Chiffinch — William Chiffinch (d. 1691)
Page of the Bedchamber and Keeper of the King's Closet 1666–88

William Chiffinch succeeded as a Page of the Bedchamber in 1666 on the death of his only brother Thomas, who had been one of Charles I's Pages of the Bedchamber from 1644. Chiffinch was also the Keeper of the King's Closet, a key post in the Household with control of the King's backstairs — in the words of Halifax Charles II had 'backstairs to convey informations to him as well as for other uses'.[40]

The Works accounts show that in 1662 his brother had lodgings at the bottom of the Queen's backstairs and also near the bakehouse.[41] However, shortly after Chiffinch succeeded him, the King had new Privy Lodgings erected on the riverside — the Volery Lodgings. It is here that the 1670 plan shows rooms (marked W) occupied by Chiffinch. Yet he still had a cellar in Scotland Yard and rooms at the Grainery.[42] As the Keeper of the Closet, in charge of the King's works of art, he removed the King's pictures and statues to the Grainery for safekeeping in 1660–1.[43]

Chiffinch is shown as occupying four rooms (the Works accounts suggest five) in the low single-storey range which made up the east (river) side of the Volery court. The rooms were set up within the Tudor riverside gallery, part of Henry VIII's final building phase at Whitehall. Both the Volery and the low range before it can be seen on views from the river (Figs. 2, 4). Little is known of his accommodation other than the fact that it had a flushing close-stool.[44] The lodging was strategically placed at the foot of the King's backstairs, physically controlling access to them and also close to the Privy Bridge guarding private river access to the King too. On two occasions Pepys describes that Chiffinch provided him with access to the King's Privy Lodgings. First in 1667 he took him to the King's closet to view the paintings and then in April 1669 Pepys records that he 'took me to the backstairs, and ther with his friend Mr. Fawkes ... he did make me ... eat a pickled herring, the largest I ever saw'.[45] After the defeat of the Duke of Monmouth at Sedgemoor in July 1685 it was in Chiffinch's lodging that the Duke had his last interview with James II to plead for his life.[46]

Presumably when not accompanying the King elsewhere or while at leisure he retired to his lodgings at the Grainery. Here new rooms were built for him at royal expense in 1669. In the 1688/9 lodging list his lodging at the Grainery is stated to have twelve rooms and another four above rented from one Captain Shales.[47]

Lady Churchill's Laundry — Lady Elizabeth Churchill
Wife of Sir Winston Churchill, the Clerk-Comptroller of the Board of the Greencloth 1664–86, Clerk of the Greencloth 1686–8

Lady Churchill was the wife of Sir Winston Churchill (d. 1688), one of the Clerks Comptrollers of the Greencloth. Their eldest surviving son, John, was the future Duke of Marlborough.

Churchill is called, in the Works accounts, 'Sir Vincent' and appears to have had a substantial lodging as would befit his position. His dining room, bedchambers, closets, study and staircase are all mentioned.[48] The Laundry which is marked 45 was located in the midst of the Queen's bakehouse near the Yeomen of the Scullery and next to a laundry belonging to Sir Thomas Clifford. The location of the two laundries may have been influenced by the opportunity to exploit the warmth of the bakehouse for heating water and drying clothes.

Mrs Churchill — Arabella Churchill (d. 1730)
Maid of Honour to the Duchess of York

Arabella Churchill, daughter of Sir Winston and Lady Churchill (q.v.) was one of the Duchess of York's Maids of Honour. After a hunting accident in the mid-1660s (which was rumoured to have been deliberate), she became the Duke of York's mistress, eventually bearing him four children. Later she married Colonel Charles Godfrey, another household official. Her position as mistress to the heir apparent is reflected by the very large lodging she occupied in Middle Scotland Yard north of the Woodyard (marked 50).

It was a whole house on at least two floors, the ground floor having seven or more rooms. Part of the same building, to the east, was the Queen's Laundry. The location of the lodging — in Scotland Yard — is interesting, both in terms of her concubinage and an illustration of the increasingly residential use of Scotland Yard after the household reforms of 1663.

Clerk of the Works — William Dickinson (d. 1702)
Chief Clerk of the King's Works and Clerk Ingrosser, 1660–1702

Unlike the better known architect and draftsman William Dickinson (jun.) who was probably his son, William Dickinson the elder was only a writing clerk. As Chief Clerk he had the responsibility of keeping the accounts of the Office of Works. His lodging, marked 64 on Vertue's plan, was part of a row of Office of Works buildings and was immediately adjacent to that of the Comptroller of the Works, Sir Hugh May, who was responsible for the financial management of the Office. On his death in 1702 Dickinson was succeeded by Sir Christopher Wren's son, Christopher Junior.[49]

The lodging which Dickinson occupied was built or rebuilt in 1660–1 and was a self-contained building on two floors with a brick stair. The 1670 plan shows it as having five rooms at ground-floor level and the 1689 lodging list tells us that it had eight rooms and three closets.[50]

Sir Thomas Clifford's Kitchen and Laundry — Thomas Clifford, 1st Lord Clifford of Chudleigh (d. 1673)
Treasurer of the Household, November 1668–72
See *Treasurer of the Household*

Sir Francis Clinton — Francis Clinton
Gentleman of the Privy Chamber 1669–?85

Clinton, who was knighted in 1661, was married to Elizabeth, Lady Clinton, Dresser to the Queen, from about 1666 until her death in December 1677. Lady Clinton was the daughter of Sir William Killigrew (q.v.), Vice-Chamberlain to the Queen, and it was probably through his wife that he held the lodging, as his post as Gentleman of the Privy Chamber was not sufficient in itself.[51] Indeed, the lodging, marked Y on the 1670 plan, was sited directly beneath the Queen's lodgings — a convenient location for the Queen's Dresser. It was a large apartment with at least five rooms and a large fireplace which was probably that of the Queen's Privy Kitchen.

The Cock

The Cock was a building housing a stopcock. It was a small room, numbered 40, with a fireplace in which the great stopcock was situated which controlled the water supply to the palace. It was sited immediately adjacent to the Waterhouse (q.v.) which housed the palace cisterns, number 31.

The Cofferer's Office — William Ashburnham (d. 1679)
Cofferer to the Household 1642–6 and 1660–79

Ashburnham had served as Cofferer of the Household during the Civil War and was duly reappointed to that position in 1660. The Cofferer had responsibility for paying the wages of some of the above and below stairs servants, and as such Ashburnham shared in Treasury business with Pepys who styled him an 'experienced man and a Cavalier'.[52]

His lodgings are described as the Cofferer's 'office' on Vertue's plan and numbered 47, but the Works accounts call the rooms his 'lodgings'. The rooms were at the north end of the small beer buttery, just off the Woodyard overlooking the Thames. They can be seen on Knyff's view (Fig. 5). In the 1688/9 lodgings list ten rooms are listed as comprising the lodging.[53]

Mr Comptroller and The Comptrollers Office — Francis Newport, 1st Earl of Bradford (d. 1708)
Comptroller of the Household 1668–87

Newport, who had been Comptroller of the Household since 1668, was one of the longest-serving senior household officers of the period. Promoted to Treasurer of the Household in 1672, he held that position until dismissed by James II in 1687 and again from 1689 until his death in 1708. He was twice advanced to the peerage, first in 1675, becoming Viscount Newport, and a second time in 1694, becoming the Earl of Bradford.

The Comptroller was the chief accountant of the Board of the Greencloth and thus a key figure in the administration of the household. He had a very large lodging with three rooms overlooking King Street and a further eight rooms on the other side of the gallery, all marked Y. This building, which can be seen on a painting of Charles II entering Whitehall (Fig. 5), was Elizabethan and of a typical plan, a series of rooms leading off a long gallery on one side. He also had two cellars, one beneath the Banqueting House and the other beneath the stairs leading up to it; one of these was awarded by a warrant of 1669.[54]

In June 1668 a warrant was issued to transfer to him the lodgings 'which his magesties Confectioner or any other officers of the confectionery doe now possess and which adioyne to the Lodgings belonging to the esquires of the body'. The 1670 plan still shows the Confectionery next door to Newport's lodging marked 25. This is because the order of 1668 did not come into effect until 1672.[55] In February 1672–3 an order was given to erect an entirely new building on the same site for the use of Newport.[56] The work was undertaken at royal expense but to Newport's design. We know little about this structure other than that it had a 'great stair' leading to his bedchamber, a laundry, a 'stilling room', a servant's eating room and that a passage ran under it linking the Great Court with Scotland Yard.[57]

Like so many senior courtiers Newport had a house in Westminster. His name appears in the poor rate assessments as occupying a house in Bridges St, Covent Garden from at least 1661.[58]

The Comptroller of ye Works — Hugh May
(d. 1684)
Comptroller of the Office of Works 1668–84

Hugh May was a leading seventeenth-century architect and one of the many Royalists rewarded at the Restoration. Paymaster of the Works from June 1668, he had hoped to succeed Sir John Denham as Surveyor, but in 1669 the surveyorship went to Sir Christopher Wren (q.v.). However, this disappointment was offset by his appointment as Surveyor of the Works at Windsor in 1674, a post which led to his greatest work, remodelling the Castle for Charles II.

The lodgings of the Comptroller lay between Great and Middle Scotland Yard in a range of buildings, mostly occupied by Works employees. They are marked on the 1670 plan (number 61) which shows them to have been a two-storey building probably with three rooms on each floor, a garden to the south and two sheds to the north. The Comptroller was responsible for the financial management of the Office of Works, and so it is appropriate that the lodging to the east was that of the Clerk of Works, William Dickinson (q.v.). Less conveniently to the west was the noxious poultry house.

The Works accounts give little detail of the lodging, but tell how, in 1674, a new closet measuring 10 ft by 6 ft was built in the little garden and a partition raised between it and his parlour. This might suggest that despite his heavy work load at Windsor and on the Commission for the Rebuilding of the City, he found it necessary to stay in Scotland Yard on occasion. After May's death in 1684 the office of Comptroller was left vacant until May 1689 and the lodging, described as being of ten rooms, was let.[59]

The Confectory — Henry Walthew
Sergeant of the Confectory from 1660[60]

In 1670 the Confectory was staffed by a Sergeant, Yeoman and a Groom and had an office next door to the Comptroller's lodging, marked 25. It seems to have comprised an outer passageway, two ground-floor rooms and, judging by the staircase, rooms above. Although marked as part of the Confectory, in 1670 these rooms had already been re-assigned to the Comptroller of the Household (q.v.). For some unknown reason this transfer did not take place until 1672.[61] In compensation in June 1688 permission was given for the Confectorer to have the rooms behind the Groom Porter's (q.v.) in which some of the 'officers do sell wine'.[62]

Captain Cooke — Thomas Cooke (d. 1697)
Master of the Tennis Courts before 1662–89

We know very little about Thomas Cooke who was appointed soon after the Restoration to the Keepership of the Tennis Courts, which had existed at Whitehall since the early 1530s. Charles II had a passion for tennis, something he had probably developed whilst in exile in France. As early as September 1660 repairs were being undertaken to the Tennis Court.[63] However, the great open court seems not to have pleased the King nearly as much as the one at Hampton Court which dated from the mid-1620s, and orders were given that this court should be copied for Whitehall.[64] The construction of the court proved over hasty, Pepys recording in his diary for 24 June 1663 'this day I observed the house which I took to be the new tennis-court, newly built next my Lord's [Monmouth's] lodgings, to be fallen down by the badness of the foundation or slight working'.[65] The finished building can be seen in the background of Vertue's view of the palace from the river (Fig. 4).

In 1666 a new staircase was built at the Tennis Court, possibly the one shown in the square building marked 'P' at the north end of the court. This almost certainly led up to a number of rooms for the King including his Dressing Room and Bedchamber.[66] In October 1677 the Bedchamber was supplied with a crimson bed, elbow chair, two stools, window curtains and a Portugal mat. Presumably to mask the odours of the King's labours, 'sweet powders and perfumes' were delivered to Cooke for the King's bedchamber at the Tennis Court the same year.[67]

The remainder of the lodgings are not particularly easy to interpret. Presumably the building at the south end of the court was Cooke's residence and the long narrow building to its east with seven rooms provided storage for the court. The position of Master of the Tennis Court was regarded as a lucrative one. The post was described in 1720 as having 'the keeping of the Tennis-Court, and the Profits which arise by playing. He has likewise the Apartments belonging to it, which yield considerable Perquisites'.[68]

The Councill Office — The Clerks of the Council

The Council Office was assigned to the four Clerks of the Council who were important figures with high status and the responsibility for compiling the registers of the Privy Council. Their offices, marked Q, were immediately beneath the Council Chamber, and connected to it by a stair. The stair cannot be identified on the 1670 plan but their six rooms can.

The Works accounts give some insight into the arrangement and working of the office. The Clerks' furniture was provided by the Office of Works who, in 1667, built a table with lockable drawers, a cupboard 7 ft high with four shelves and a collapsible table.[69] One of the rooms under the Council Chamber was called the Registers Office, where presumably the registers were stored. Another was the room 'where the clerks write'.

This room was given 'paper' (i.e. frosted) windows in 1668 to guarantee the clerks privacy.[70]

The Lord Crofts — William Crofts, 1st Lord Crofts (d. 1677)
Gentleman of the Bedchamber to the King 1666–77

William Crofts was brought up at court and before the Civil War was Master of Horse to James Duke of York. With Charles II in exile, he became responsible for educating the Duke of Monmouth after the death of his mother and was created Baron Crofts in 1658. At the Restoration he brought the Duke to England and was created Gentleman of the Bedchamber.

The Works accounts make it plain that the relatively small ground-floor lodging shown on the 1670 plan, letter M, extended to the first floor and was entered off the Matted Gallery. It was therefore one of the highest status lodgings, on the prestigious Matted Gallery and directly in communication with those of the King himself.[71]

Like most of the higher ranking courtiers Crofts had a house in Westminster. This was located in Newport Street in St Martins-in-the-Field and occupied by him from at least 1669.[72]

Colonel Darcye — the Hon. Marmaduke Darcy (d. 1687)
Gentleman Usher of the King's Privy Chamber 1660–87

Marmaduke Darcy was one of the companions of Charles II's exile, holding the office of Gentleman Usher of the Privy Chamber. At the Restoration, he returned to England on the ship transporting the King and was immediately made a Gentleman Usher of the King's Privy Chamber and later (in 1673) Surveyor of the Great Wardrobe. As Gentleman Usher Darcy qualified for his own lodging as well as the use of the room for the Gentlemen of the Privy Chamber (q.v.). His lodging, marked N, was on the ground floor of the Tilt-yard Gallery at its west end and comprised three rooms.

Doctor of the Household — Dr Thomas Waldron (d. 1677)
Physician to the Household 1667–77

Thomas Waldron was appointed Physician to the 'King's person and Household' in August 1667 and the same month he was granted the lodgings of his predecessor Dr Clarke.[73] The lodging is marked 31 on the 1670 plan and comprises a number of small rooms squeezed in between those of the King's Apothecary, John Chase (q.v.) and the Groom Porter (q.v.). It appears from the plan as if access to his rooms was only through those of the Apothecary.

Within a year of obtaining his post, Waldron moved into a house on the east side of Bridges Street in Covent Garden, taking a house previously occupied by one Dr Torlesse. This may have been for his family or to enable him to run a private practice too.[74]

Mr Dupper — Sir Thomas Duppa (d. 1694)
Assistant Gentleman Usher Daily Waiter 1662–71

There were four Gentlemen Ushers Daily Waiters, the most senior of whom held the post of Gentleman Usher of the Black Rod, an officer of the Order of the Garter. Black Rod had a separate, slightly larger, lodging whilst the other three gentlemen had rooms close together on the first floor which do not show on the 1670 plan. The 1688/9 lodgings list lists the three others as having two rooms and a closet each.[75] Duppa started his career as a Gentleman Usher Quarter Waiter and was promoted to an Assistant Gentleman Usher Daily Waiter in 1662 with the promise of a position as a full Gentleman as soon as there was a vacancy.[76] In 1671 Duppa was promoted, and with his promotion came improved lodgings.

On the Antiquaries' plan he is styled Mr Duppa (he was knighted in 1683) and his lodging (number 56) appears to have been a single room entered from Scotland Yard with a single fireplace. At the time he was an Assistant Gentleman Usher Daily Waiter. However on 19 February 1671 he was promoted to a full Gentleman which he remained through three reigns until his death in April 1694. The warrant for his promotion states that he was to be granted the lodging formerly occupied by Sir James Mercer his predecessor, who had recently died. A further warrant, a week later, authorized the Sergeant at Arms to move into Duppa's former lodging[77] and in the Works accounts for January 1671 there is an item for blocking up doors in the lodging which Mr Duppa 'formerly had'. In subsequent years repair accounts tell us that he was assigned a top-floor lodging at the north end of the Banqueting House.[78] The 1688–9 lodging list refers to this lodging as his 'former lodging now in the occupation of Lady Osborne', but this must have been a temporary measure as a repair reference in November 1689 confirms that he still occupied it.[79]

The fact that Duppa was given a separate and larger lodging than the other gentlemen confirms that he was Black Rod. As Black Rod, in 1683, he rented his lodgings to the King for the accommodation of Lord Howard of Escrick for 20s. a week.[80]

Mr. Early — *probably* Robert Ernle
Gentleman of the Buttery 1660–78[81]

The Ernle family were associated with the Buttery and Queen's Cellar throughout Charles II's reign. Robert Ernle was the Gentleman of the Buttery and had two Yeomen and two Grooms working under him. Two Butteries are marked on the 1670 plan, the Privy Buttery, in the traditional location north of the Great Hall, and the Small Beer Buttery, on the river front, not far from Ernle's lodging marked 43 on the plan. Ernle occupied one room on the north side of the range housing the Scalding House and Yeomen of the Woodyard. The other Buttery staff would have lodged in the Buttery buildings.

Elliot, Thomas Killigrew (q.v.), Richard Lane, Robert Phillips, Silius Titus, David Walter, Edward Progers, William Legge, the Hon. Henry Coventry and James Hamilton.[102]

Although only Thomas Killigrew appears on the 1670 plan, it is known from the Lord Chamberlain's warrants and the Works accounts that at least three of the others had lodgings at Whitehall. In 1661 Thomas Elliot had the window of his lodging damaged by the King's pleasure boat: in 1678 the accounts tell us that Elliot's 'old lodging' was beneath the Duke of York's Presence Chamber.[103] In 1676 Richard Lane had a lodging over the Court Gate with a garret and an eating room which led into his bedchamber.[104] Henry Coventry stood down as Gentleman when he was appointed Secretary of State in June 1672; as Secretary of State in 1677 he had an office near the council chamber.[105]

The suggestion that lodging number 5 was occupied by the Grooms of the Privy Bedchamber is supported by several references in the Works accounts to 'the Groomes of ye bedchambers Dineing roome at ye kings backstaires'.[106] The Gentlemen of the Privy Bedchamber had rooms at the top of the backstairs nearby.[107]

The Groomes of ye Privy chamber — Grooms of the Privy Chamber

During Charles II's reign there were six Grooms of the Privy Chamber whose duties were entirely honorific. They had no daily duties or attendance except on extraordinary occasions such as embassies and coronations.[108] In 1670 these six Grooms were Maurice Wynn, James Elliott, Robert Thompson, Adrian May, James Progers and Thomas Ross,[109] none of whom apparently had lodgings in their own right.

The rooms which they occupied whilst on duty were numbered 21 and seem to have been on two floors as a staircase is shown. The lodgings were close to those of the Officers of the Jewel House and the Gentlemen of the Privy Chamber.

His Royal Highness — James, Duke of York
(d. 1701)
Brother of Charles II and future King James II

On his return to Whitehall at the Restoration, Charles II was accompanied by his brother, the Duke of York, the future James II. Although it is not certain where he lodged in 1660, he may have had rooms in or under the Turks' Gallery (a first-floor gallery near the Queen's Lodgings). Certainly by late 1664 he was installed in the Prince's Lodgings overlooking the Thames at the south end of the Privy

Garden.[110] Anne Hyde, who married the Duke in September 1660, seems initially to have had rooms immediately adjoining the Queen's Lodgings, which she retained after her marriage, but on the arrival of Catherine of Braganza in 1662 she gave these up, joining the Duke in the Prince's Lodgings by 1664.[111]

In May 1664 Hugh May received a warrant for £300 towards repairs in the Prince's Lodgings, and a month later an extraordinary account was opened for what turned out to be their complete refurbishment for the Duke.[112] The so-called Prince's Lodgings had first been built by Henry VIII for Princess Mary and had, before the Civil War, been occupied by close members of the royal family. The use to which the rooms were put during the Republic is unclear, but on the eve of the Restoration General Monck (the Duke of Albemarle q.v.) was occupying them. They were substantially repaired and altered for the Duke of York. After the Tudor coping stones on the battlements had been removed, the Matted Gallery behind the lodging was encased in scaffolding and raised one storey higher in brick to provide new rooms on the west side of the Prince's Lodgings. The new buildings can be seen on a painting of 1683 lying behind the Tudor building which they completely dominate (Fig. 8). The accounts list a complete set of outer rooms starting with a guard chamber which was approached by 'a great stair', a presence chamber, a privy chamber, a bedchamber (with bed alcove), a dressing room, a closet and an oratory.[113] Likewise the Duchess was provided with a guard chamber, presence chamber, privy chamber, withdrawing room, bedchamber (also with a bed alcove), dressing room and closet. Her closet was in one of the Tudor turrets which lay next to her little bedchamber. The two sets of apartments interconnected via a passage which ran between the Duke's dressing room and the Duchess's bedchamber.[114] After the initial creation of the two sets of lodgings further alterations were made in 1665–6 and again in 1670. In 1670 the Duchess's drawing room was divided horizontally, and a closet created in the new upper space, superseding the closet in a turret. The lower room was converted into a bedchamber, while the original bedchamber became a withdrawing room. The windows in the old turret and several other Tudor casements facing the Thames were replaced with sashes.[115] The new windows can be seen on the painting of 1683 (Fig. 8). Access to the ducal apartments was either by the Great Stair leading to his Guard Chamber (for the less important or less intimate) or via the refitted Matted Gallery directly connecting with the Vane Room and the King's bedchamber.

The Duchess died in March 1671 and her rooms together with the Duke's remained unchanged until shortly before the Duke's second marriage in September 1673 to Mary of Modena. Then the Sergeant Painter was paid for sprucing up the Duchess's rooms, and building work began on a new bedchamber for the couple and an oratory.[116] In August 1675 soon after the birth of her short-lived first child, Catherine Laura, work started on the enlargement of the new Duchess's oratory and the redesign of her closet and stoolroom.[117] For three years from March 1679 when the Duke was in the Netherlands and Scotland, his lodgings remained largely empty, but on the eve of his return, minor repairs were undertaken and work began on the construction of a new closet next to his Guard Chamber.[118]

The Duke's lodgings are only fully shown on the Vertue version of the 1670 plan where they are marked B. The ground-floor rooms occupy the entire river frontage of the old Prince's Lodgings, at least eighteen rooms, and another eleven rooms and a courtyard off the Stone Gallery. It is not possible to identify with certainty any of the rooms, which presumably belonged to the Duke and Duchess's large household.

Mr Hyde — Laurence Hyde, 1st Earl of Rochester (d. 1711)
Master of the King's Robes May 1662–78

Laurence Hyde was the son of Charles II's Lord Chancellor, the Earl of Clarendon, and the brother of Anne Hyde, Duchess of York. In 1670 he was still plain Mr Hyde holding the post of Master of the King's Robes, but in 1682 he was created Earl of Rochester and went on to be Lord Treasurer under James II. As Master of the Robes he was responsible for managing all the royal clothing and much ceremonial dress. In practice the work of the office was delegated to a clerk whose staff were a Wardrobe Keeper, a Yeoman, three grooms, a page and a brusher.

A number of repair accounts establish the location of the office of the King's Robes hard up against the west side of the Stone Gallery in the Privy Garden, and a lodging within it for the Master of the Robes.[119] Before the Civil War the King's Robes had been sited at the backstairs and although it is not known precisely when they moved premises, it was probably undertaken in 1660. The lodging, marked S on the 1670 plan, was very small with what seems to have been a great bay window overlooking the Privy Garden and its own private walled garden to the north and south.

In July 1678 Sidney Godolphin, a former Groom of the Bedchamber (q.v.) became Master of the Robes in Hyde's stead. Godolphin swapped his lodging with that of Baptist May, Keeper of the Privy Purse, who wished to rebuild at his own expense the lodgings assigned to the Master of the Robes.[120] This he did, creating a fine little house overlooking the Privy Garden. The lodgings list of 1688/9 lists the new accommodation as four rooms and two garrets.[121] The lodging was completely destroyed in the fire of 1691.

Madam Charlotte Killigrew — Charlotte Killigrew (d. c. 1716)
First Lady of the Queen's Privy Chamber from 1662

Madam Charlotte Killigrew, as she is described both on the 1670 plan and in the Works accounts, married the dramatist Thomas Killigrew in 1655 at the Hague. Killigrew and his brother, Sir William Killigrew (q.v.), both entered the King's Privy Chamber in 1660. Both husband and wife rose high in royal service. In 1673 Killigrew succeeded Henry Herbert as Master of the Revels, and Charlotte was at first appointed Keeper of the Sweet Coffers for the Queen and then in June 1662 First Lady of the Queen's Privy Chamber.[122] It was in this capacity that she was awarded a lodging at Whitehall.

Charlotte's lodgings are marked E on the key to the 1670 plan, but do not appear on any of the three versions of it. The Works accounts have only three references to Madam Killigrew's lodgings, but mention those of her husband more than a dozen times. References to Charlotte's lodgings describe them as being adjacent to the Queen's backstairs and 'the backstairs leading to the king's waiters'.[123] Thomas Killigrew's rooms are described in the same terms so we can be sure that they occupied the same quarters as husband and wife.[124] A warrant of 1682 in connection with the reconstruction of the Queen's backstairs mention 'the Lady Killigrewes entry or passage into her lodgings' and this confirms that still, at this date, the lodgings were in the same area.[125]

The approximate location of the Queen's backstairs is known from the Works accounts, although not shown on the 1670 plan. They were just off the passage from the Pebble Court shown, without wash, as a right of way on the Vertue plan.[126] This passage does not appear on the other two versions of the plan, and this omission is one of the very few points of significant discrepancy between the extant versions. Coupled with this anomaly there are a small number of unattributed lodgings beneath the King's and Queen's apartments near this passage, particularly the rooms next to the Queen's Waiters (I) and the Queen's Wardrobe (D) and another group next to the Countess of Falmouth (H). This seems to indicate that for some reason this part of the plan is incomplete and that Madam Killigrew's Lodgings were omitted in this area.

Sir Philip Killigrew, *probably* Sir Peter Killigrew
Gentleman of the Privy Chamber in Waiting, 1660–89

Even though Sir Philip Killigrew's name appears both on the Lansdowne MS list and the Vertue and Antiquaries' plans, his Christian name was almost certainly Peter. Sir Peter Killigrew born c. 1634, the only surviving son and heir of Sir Peter Killigrew (d. 1668). Both Sir Peter elder and younger were Gentlemen of the Privy Chamber. This presumption receives corroboration from two references in the Works accounts to the lodgings of Sir Peter Killigrew at the Cockpit. One of these tells us that his lodgings were situated on two floors and adjoined the Duke of Albemarle's (q.v.) lodgings.[127]

On the 1670 plan the lodgings are marked 'O' and are shown on the Cockpit side next to the Duke of Monmouth's lodgings and not far from the Duke of Albermarle's. One large room is shown and two small ones. The lodging would have been entered off the passage to the park.

ng in August 1670 when a desk
re and foundations were dug.[203]
d was an older building and can
e views of Whitehall from St
e principal lodge was immedi-
queting House occupying the
Gate. The 1688/9 lodgings list
ised four rooms.[204] It is men-
everal times, and in 1669 there is
d 'filling up with bars' to make
cords with the porter's duty of
ourt.[205]

— Simon Ager

the Poultry, Simon Ager, there
rooms, a Purveyor and a Clerk.
0 on the 1670 plan, had four
loor, a staircase and a garden.
oddly squeezed in amongst the
of Works. In addition to the
er ran the Scalding House (q.v.)
e prepared and stored.

Povey (d. 1705)
85

M.P. during the Long Parliament
became Treasurer and Receiver
York, an appointment he kept
e was made Master of Requests
e death of Charles II.
arked T on the key to the 1670
pear on the actual plan. In 1665
e Duke of York in his capacity
that year gives permission for
easuring 11 ft by 24 ft in a court
gs with a distinct entrance from
vould not be confused with the
building of these dimensions
against the Stone Gallery in the
e Prince's Lodgings. This was,

at Whitehall, Povey had two
n Fields where he entertained
gst many others.

nd seen clearly on views of the
Figs. 2, 4, 8), the Privy Kitchen
rdinal Wolsey in the 1520s and
e until the destruction of the
f it was excavated in 1939.[207] It
ion that the small room to the
d western wall, was a stair con-
e royal apartments.

Quarter Waiters

There were eight Gentlemen Ushers Quarter Waiters who had the duty to wait in the Presence Chamber in pairs and assist the Gentlemen Ushers Daily Waiters in their duties.[208] The lodging which was assigned to those on duty is numbered 23 on the 1670 plan, and comprised three or four dark rooms off a narrow passage next to the Signet and Privy Seal Office (24).

In 1665 their lodging was refurbished by the Office of Works. Other work commissioned independently gave rise to a complaint which Charles II referred to Sir Christopher Wren: 'Whereas his magesties Gentlemen Ushers Quarter Wayters have caused to be erected a building without my leave which is a very great annoyance to ye Master of his Magesties Jewell house, These are therefore to pray ... you to cause the same to forthwith pulled downe that it noe further prejudice to ye said Master of ye Jewell house'.[209] Presumably the Gentlemen had built up against the Jewel House (number 22) to the west obstructing their light. Five years later a fence with a gate in it was erected in front of their lodging.[210]

The Queen's Secretary — Sir Richard Bellings
(d. 1716)
The Queen's Secretary from 1663

Bellings was secretary to Catherine of Braganza and was knighted in 1666. According to the 1670 plan his lodging, Letter K, was in the northern section of the Tudor Privy Kitchen range on the waterfront. Only one large room is shown and a Vice stair which service presumably led up to more rooms above. Two floors can be seen on views of the palace from the river (Fig. 5). The Works accounts show that his floor had to be raised by loads of rubbish to prevent it from being flooded.[211]

The Queen's Waiters

It is not entirely clear who the Queen's Waiters were. In 1663 Charles II had set out that the Queen should have five Gentlemen Ushers Daily Waiters, five Daily Waiters and Six Quarter Waiters.[212] The rooms for the Queen's Waiters are given both the letter I and the number 8 on the key to the 1670 plan. Number 8 does not appear but I is a group of seven rooms located between the King's Pages of the King's Backstairs and the Queen's Wardrobe. This location is confirmed by references in the Works accounts.[213] They were conveniently sited for easy access to the Queen's Lodgings above for any of the groups of Waiters who might have been stationed there.

The Duke of Richmond — Charles Stuart,
3rd Duke of Richmond and 6th Duke of Lennox
(d. 1672)
Great Chamberlain of Scotland 1660–72

As Earl of Lichfield Charles Stuart took part in the Royalist rising in 1659, and shortly after the Restoration he succeeded his cousin as 3rd Duke of Richmond. Richmond made a habit of courting royal favour despite a number of spectacular disagreements with the King. Of these Richmond's elopement and third marriage in March 1667 was the most serious. Charles II had let it be known that he would like a divorce to enable him to marry Frances Stuart (1648–1702), who until then had been one of his mistresses. Catherine of Braganza acted as an intermediary to reconcile the Richmonds with the King, and in 1668 swore the Duchess as one of her Bedchamber. The Richmonds were granted a house in the Bowling Green at Whitehall. It is this building which is marked D on the 1670 plan.

Richmond had had lodgings at Whitehall since 1661 when he was granted the former lodgings of Sir Thomas Jermyn.[214] It is not known when he vacated these nor when he moved into the house on the Bowling Green. The Bowling Green house had originally been leased to Sir Charles Berkeley in January 1662, and it was from the roof of this 'new erected house of building brick' that in August 1662 Pepys saw the arrival of Charles II and Catherine of Braganza shortly after their marriage.[215]

In February 1666 a warrant for the erection of a fence between the Watergate, shown at the north-east corner of the Bowling Green, and the Duke's house establishes his occupancy. He seems to have begun to extend the building immediately, and an item in his household accounts suggests that work was underway that April.[216] It is in this form that the 1670 plan shows Richmond House because two years later a warrant to the Surveyor of Works directs the house to be extended 'as his grace shall direct'. After the Duke's death in 1672 the duchess continued to live in the house until her own death in 1702. The 1688/9 lodgings list states that the house, at that time, had twenty-eight rooms.[217]

Prince Rupert — Count Palatine of the Rhine and Duke of Bavaria (d. 1682)
The King's Cousin

Charles II's cousin, Prince Rupert, was the third son of Elizabeth, Queen of Bohemia. At the Restoration he was granted a pension of £6,000 a year and lodgings at Whitehall, which he occupied until his death in 1682. In October 1661 a warrant instructed the Office of Works to prepare the former lodgings of the Earl of Norwich for the Prince. Thus the lodgings are described as 'new' in the Works accounts of March 1662, with a ground and first floor, and a second floor lit by dormers. They were on the west side of the Stone Gallery approached via the Matted Gallery.[218] The 1670 survey confirms that they were on the opposite side of the Gallery to the lodgings of the Duke of York and marks them C.

In 1671 they were extended and refitted to comprise at least a dining room, a bedroom with an ante-room, a pantry, a laboratory and cellars.[219] On 22 June 1672 an order was given to Wren to erect a building 30 ft wide next to the Stone Gallery in the Privy Garden 'betweene the Robes and his highnesse Prince Rupert's Lodgings' and an extraordinary account opened three months later describes the construction of a building with cellars, a new bedchamber and closet.[220]

The Scalding House

The Scalding House was where poultry were plunged into boiling water to aid plucking. In 1670 it was under the jurisdiction of a Yeoman, Grooms and Pages, six staff in all.[221] There was no Sergeant of the Scalding House probably because the Sergeant of the Poultry (q.v.) had overall control. This makes it very likely that the Scalding House, number 41, was a workhouse and the administration of the supply and preparation of birds for table would have been carried on from the Poultry Office, number 60.

The Scullery and Yeomen of the Sculleries

Lodgings were provided for any of the three Yeomen of the Scullery as they came into waiting. In 1670 the Yeomen were John Lander, first Yeoman; Thomas Tooth, second Yeoman; and William Lloyd, third Yeoman.[222] The Scullery, marked 12 on the plan, was conveniently sited behind the Household Kitchen to wash and clean all the King's plate, pewter and other things used at table. There were six rooms and the Works accounts indicate that in 1695 there was a lodging above allocated to Sir William Forrester's Gentleman.[223]

Lady Sears — Catherine, Lady Sayers (d. ?1685)
Dresser, Starcher and Laundress to the Queen, 1681–?5

Catherine Sayers was the widow of Sir John Sayers, who had been Page to the Prince of Orange and Colonel of Foot. Sayers's father, Sir George, had been Master of the Horse to Elizabeth, Queen of Bohemia. Following Sayers's death in September 1667, Catherine obtained a continuance for life of her husband's pension of £200 a year. Lodgings at Whitehall may have been another expression of favour to her or her husband. In the closing years of the reign she became a Dresser to the Queen.[224] Her lodging is marked as Q on the 1670 plan lying on the west side of the Bowling Green.

In 1679 Lady Sayers was ordered to surrender her lodging in favour of Philip Kirke, son of George Kirke (q.v.), Keeper of the Palace 1663–9. Philip Kirke had succeeded to his father's former post that year and wished to build himself a new lodging to the east of Lady Sayers' which would have engulfed hers.[225] Evidently Kirke's plans were frustrated as the house was still in her name in 1687 and seems to have remained so

, in 1734, her former lodgings,
 the fires of 1691 and 1698,
d ruinous' and as having been
her death.[226]

lan, these buildings were part

eal Office — Clerks of the

Clerks of the Signet and Privy
r and from at least 1689 they
he four Clerks of the Signet
es of State and those of the
Privy Seal who, in 1670, was
Their tasks were administra-
ts and collecting fees for doing
iet but this was removed and
wages.[227] The Clerks occupied
 between the Officers of the
gings of the Quarter Waiters
 plan.

ly de Silvius (née la Garde)

70

fe of the diplomat Sir Gabriel
r to Catherine of Braganza.
ed to Lady Silvius on her own
ueen, a post for which she was
board wages of £60 a year.[228]
as a substantial one, is marked
stood beneath the King's Pres-
a warrant was issued for the
 closet next to Lady Silvius's
's Waiters rooms with a chim-
 make it clear that it was next
t had two brick drains beneath
a garderobe.[229] The warrant
as 'for the Queen's use', but
e no doubt that it was part of

Barbara Howard (d. 1681)
ueen 1661–81

lk was the daughter of Sir
idow of the Hon. Richard
d the 3rd Earl Suffolk during
 1662 the Countess was desig-
 Stool, first lady of the Bed-
 the Robes and Keeper of the
of Braganza. At the same time
 lodging on two floors in the

heart of the King's and Queen's apartments. Marked on
the 1670 plan as 'C', the lodgings were sandwiched
between the Stone Gallery and the King's Privy Lodgings (the Volery). The part immediately adjacent to the
Volery was single storey with a lead flat. During the construction of the Volery in 1666, this part was shored up
and repaired.[230] The part adjacent to the Stone Gallery
was part of what was probably a Jacobean lodging leading onto the Matted Gallery and was approached by a
great stair.[231]

The Countess's lodgings underwent continual
improvement during the reign. In July 1669 a warrant
authorized the dismantling of her old backstairs and the
construction of 'such roomes for the countesse of
Suffolke as her ladyshipp shall informe you shalbe convenient for her and the place will beare'.[232] Only two
years later, in December 1671, an extraordinary account
lists works done at the Countess's 'new' lodgings.[233] The
accounts are unclear as to the extent of this work, but it
seems to have been an improvement of the existing
rooms rather than a move to new ones. After the death
of the Countess in 1681, the Works accounts refer to
the lodging as her 'old' lodgings and in March 1682 the
whole area was cleared for the construction of the
King's new lodgings. In 1667 the Countess was given an
extra little single storey room in the garden with a bird-
cage in it.[234]

The Surveyor and the Surveyor Office —
Sir Christopher Wren (d. 1723)
Surveyor of the King's Works 1669–1718

Sir Christopher Wren moved
into the Surveyor's official
lodgings immediately upon
his appointment in 1669.
These unusually large
buildings together with
the Surveyor's Office
were at the easternmost
end of a range of building
almost entirely given over
to Works offices and are
marked as 57 and 58 on the
1670 plan. The lodging and office
of the Surveyor General of the King's Works seems
only to have been located in this position since the
Restoration, Inigo Jones's lodgings evidently having
been situated in the far north-west corner of Scotland
Yard.[235]

The building was of two storeys with attics and a
great stair leading to the first floor. The rooms mentioned in the Works accounts are the little dining room
and the great dining room, the 'alcove room' or bedchamber which was panelled and led into a dressing
room, the withdrawing room and a closet. We also know
that only a door separated Wren's lodging from the
Office of the Works itself.[236] In addition to the lodging
there was a little garden where a seat was made, sur-
mounted by a pediment.[237] The 1689 lodgings list tells

us that the lodging comprised, in all, sixteen rooms and a cellar.[238]

On his dismissal from office in 1718, extraordinarily, for a man who had spent almost all of his professional life safeguarding the King's interest against that of greedy courtiers, Wren was ordered to return certain fittings of the lodgings which he had allegedly removed.[239]

The Sutlers

The Sutlery, which sold provisions to the army, was rebuilt in 1687 to make it larger and provide lodgings for the Major who ran it.[240] In 1670, numbered 3, and up against the Charcoal house, it can have been little more than a series of sheds.

The Treasury Chambers — Sir George Downing
(d. 1684)
Secretary to the Treasury 1667–71

Sir George Downing was a former Parliamentarian who, through his talents, rose to high office under Charles II becoming Secretary to the Treasury Commissioners in 1667. Downing was to play a significant role in the development of the Treasury as an Office of State. Sited next to the lodgings of the Lord Keeper and the Lord Chamberlain and immediately below the King's innermost lodgings and the Council Chamber, the Treasury Chambers comprised eight rooms marked S. The two largest were on the Privy Garden front with its outer walls coloured blue on the 1670 plan. The whole of this large office was the territory of the Secretary to the Treasury and his entourage. These included, in 1670, the Solicitor to the Treasury, three Clerks, the Sergeant at Arms, a Messenger to the Chamber and four Messengers of Receipt.[241]

The Works accounts give some insight into the workings of the Treasury Chambers. We learn that there was a room where the 'commissioners sit', used by the Commissioners of the Treasury, and another where the 'clerks write'. The complex was entered by a 'private passage', the location of which is unclear.[242] Vertue's plan alone shows an independent front door to the Chambers from the Privy Garden, and if his version is accurate, it is likely that this office, like Arlington's (q.v.), was publicly entered from the Privy Garden. As with the Council Office (q.v.), the Office of Works provided furniture and fittings. These included 'a board to putt orders on to hang in ye roome where the Lords cormisioners sitts', 'pinns to hang clokes on' and a board 'to keepe papers from falling downe'.[243]

The Treasurer's Office and Sir Thomas Clifford's Kitchen and Laundry — Thomas Clifford, 1st Lord Clifford of Chudleigh (d. 1673)
Treasurer of the Household, November 1668–72

Clifford rose to high office in the service of Charles II through his friendship with Lord Arlington. Appointed Comptroller of the Household and a Privy Councillor

in 1666, he went on to become Treasurer of the Household and a Treasury Commissioner. By the early 1670s he was acting as a key advisor in most major policy decisions; he knew, for instance, of the secret clauses in the Treaty of Dover. His rewards came in April 1672 when he was appointed Lord Treasurer and was raised to the peerage. This success was short-lived. Probably already on the verge of conversion to Rome, he felt unable to conform to the Test Act and so resigned from all his offices. He died soon after probably by his own hand.

The 1670 plan marks the location of his Office (number 28), kitchen (numbered 11), Laundry (number 44) and cellar. Clifford was one of the officers of the Household who was granted an office for the discharge of his duties. The Office was in the northern part of the Elizabethan range which housed the office of the Comptroller of the Household (q.v.) and the office of Sir John Trevors (q.v.). Clifford's lodgings themselves are not marked on the plan as they were at first-floor level, but the Works accounts provide some useful information. Soon after Clifford was appointed Comptroller of the Household in 1666, the Office of Works set up a lodging for his use. It is not possible to locate this, but it had a balcony, dining room, bedchamber, closet, ante-room, alcove room, withdrawing room, great stair and cellar. In other words it was one of the largest and best appointed lodgings in the palace. It is not known whether he retained this lodging on becoming Treasurer. It was refurbished a second time in late 1671.[244]

Clifford was one of the beneficiaries of the Household Reforms of 1663 whereby various courtiers and court officials were granted the use of former kitchens and offices. Clifford's kitchen seems to have been set up in the former Ewery, an old Tudor building; he also had a laundry in part of the Queen's bakehouse (number 44) which was next to that of Lady Churchill (q.v.).

Clifford was one of the high ranking courtiers who also maintained a house in Westminster. He had a house on the north side of Pall Mall at the east end from at least 1667.[245]

Sir John Trevors — Sir John Trevor (d. 1672)
Secretary of State 1668–72

Sir John Trevor was a member of Cromwell's Council of State in the months leading up to the Restoration and made his name in Charles II's diplomatic service. On his return from Paris in 1668 he was knighted and made Secretary of State.

The 1670 plan shows his lodgings, numbered 27, as occupying four rooms in the long Elizabethan range facing King Street which contained the Treasurer's Office (28) and the Comptroller (Y). In 1670 his lodgings and all those between him and the Whitehall gate were re-tiled.[246]

The Ushers Larder

This lodging is problematic as the Restoration Court was full of Gentlemen Ushers and it is unclear to whom

s marked 15 on the 1670 plan
e other larders. It may possibly
food destined for the table of
aily Waiters.

ther George or John Vaux
660

ify with any certainty. One Mr
sioner mentioned in the Duke
books as having died in 1676,
t have had a lodging at White-
at Vosse was a corruption of
Vaux were Under-Housekeep-
 or Vaux occupied five rooms
Mr Lightfoot (q.v.) and the

Sir Edward Walker (d. 1677)
-77

Walker as a secretary during the
d Charles II into exile where he
Clerk to the Privy Council. His
ollege of Arms originated in
displaced Edward Bysshe, the
as Garter King at Arms. As
 significant part in organizing
monial at court under Charles
lodgings at Whitehall beneath
arked on the 1670 plan as R.
on which enabled Walker to be
 possible to the Garter cere-
ch utilized the Council Cham-
were employed in 'putting up
Sr Edw. Walkers closset, under
ing up the seale there & putting
on'.[249] During the Great Fire of
666 Walker was responsible for
ry at the College of Arms and
ll. By 1670 the library had been
 Palace.[250]

cis Rogers
Keeper of the Standing Wardrobe

 wardrobes at Whitehall in 1670
e housed in the rooms marked
 northern part of the ground
e, were used by the Whitehall
is was inventoried in 1675 as
harles II to ensure it was better
ts were fully listed. There were
tile hangings, curtains, carpets,
ose stools, beds and bedclothes
e Chapel Royal. All these were
g of Whitehall and were quite
ving Wardrobe, Great Wardrobe
e Robes.[251]

The Standing Wardrobe had one very large room, presumably for housing large furnishing textiles and a number of smaller rooms which included a long narrow space possibly for tapestry. Rogers answered for the Wardrobe to the Lord Chamberlain.

The Water House — Peter Brent
Sergeant Plummer 1661–70

This two-room structure, number 39, was sited next to the Great Cock, number 40, and either supported or contained the palace water cisterns filled by water piped from springs in the area of modern Soho and St James's. The Sergeant Plumber, Peter Brent (held office 1661–76), had responsibility for both the Water House and the Cock and for safeguarding the palace water supply. In 1671, at Wren's insistence and on Brent's recommendation, unlicensed building was stopped in Soho as it was interfering with the palace water supply.[252]

Sir Henry Wood — Sir Henry Wood (d. 1671)
First Clerk of the Greencloth 1661–71

Wood was a courtier from a family of courtiers entering the service of Prince Charles in 1623. He was knighted at Oxford during the Civil War. Wood had been Clerk-Comptroller of the Board of the Greencloth since 1644 and was made First Clerk of the Greencloth in 1661. He was also a member of the Queen's council from 1662. His second wife, Mary, was a dresser and Woman of the Bedchamber to Catherine of Braganza.

The 1670 plan shows Sir Henry Wood's lodging in Scotland Yard (number 18), but references in the Works accounts which refer to his lodging and that of Lady Wood, dating from the early 1660s, suggest that their lodgings were originally beneath those of the Queen — 'at the queenes backstaires', 'under ye queenes presence'.[253]

Wood's lodging comprised at least five rooms, probably more. In 1662 the Cofferer paid out £300 to build three new rooms for Lady Wood in compensation for three rooms she had given over to him for a meat larder.[254] Some of the rooms on the 1670 plan may be these.

Yeomen of the Woodyard

Three Yeomen were appointed to the Woodyard in 1660 but their number was reduced to two in 1664 and finally one in 1673. In 1670 the two Yeomen were Thomas Hook and Edward Siston.[255] The Woodyard was a large walled area with a gateway on the west side of Scotland Yard. The task of the Woodyard was to provide the King's Lodgings with wood for burning and adjoining offices carried out similar functions. It was close to the King's Coalyard, the Duke of York's Woodyard and to the bakehouses which burnt considerable quantities of timber. The lodging, or office, is marked 42 on the 1670 plan. One room evidently overlooked the gate, thereby preventing the unauthorized removal of fuel. Other buildings, on the edge of the Duke's woodyard, were perhaps workshops.

Notes to Gazetteer

1. *SOL*, vol. XIII, p. 80.

2. H. J. M. Green and S. J. Thurley, 'Excavations on the West Side of Whitehall 1960–62', *London and Middlesex Archaeological Society Transactions* (1990), pp. 78, 103–5.

3. PRO Work 5/1, fo. 141.

4. *Pepys*, vol. VIII, p. 499.

5. L. E. Tanner, 'Lord High Almoners and Sub-Almoners', *Journal of the British Archaeological Association*, vol. XX, (1957–8), pp. 79, 81; *DNB*; *ORH*, pp. 56–7.

6. E. and J. Chamberlayne, *Angliae Notitia; or the Present State of England* (London, 1669), p. 243.

7. PRO Work 5/37, fo. 68.

8. PRO Work 5/25, fos. 44, 57.

9. *DNB*.

10. For Arlington's office see A. Marshall, 'Sir Joseph Williamson and the Conduct of Administration in Restoration England', *Historical Research*, vol. LXIX (1996), pp. 21–5. I am grateful to Andrew Barclay for pointing this out to me.

11. PRO Work 5/4, ff. 45–45v, 46v–47, 101, 123, 144v; PRO Work 5/3, f. 128v; PRO Work 5/19, f. 127v.

12. PRO Work 5/13, f. 69v, 118; PRO Work 5/15, fo. 24.

13. PRO LC5/147, p. 70.

14. *SOL*, vol. XIII, p. 72.

15. WCA MS. F1111.

16. BL Harl. MS. 4718.

17. PRO Work 5/29, fo. 122.

18. PRO Work 5/19, fo. 37.

19. *DNB*; Harvey Kearsley, *His Majesty's Bodyguard of the Honourable Corps of Gentlemen at Arms* (London, 1937), pp. 22–3, 87–91.

20. WCA MS F1111.

21. Robert Bucholz identifed this resident for me. Other possibilities include Daniel Bryan who was a scenekeeper for the Theatre Royal (PRO LC3/73, fo. 133), James Bryan who had a house in Westminster in St Martin's Lane (WCA MS F1099) and John Bryan an officer of the Cellar who died in 1670 (PRO LS13/252, p. 89).

22. *SOL*, vol. XVI, p. 169. This view is confirmed by later property leases.

23. *SOL*, vol. XVI, p. 168.

24. *SOL*, vol. XIII, pp. 233–4.

25. *Pepys*, vol. IV, pp. 1, 132.

26. PRO Work 5/4, fo. 145.

27. PRO LC5/138, p. 361.

28. PRO Work 5/9, ff. 47v, 56v, 58, 89v, 115v, 116.

29. PRO Work 5/10, ff.31v, 74, 75v, 83v.

30. PRO Work 5/37, f. 36v, 45.

31. BL Lansdowne MS. 736, fo. 13.

32. PRO LS13/252, p. 48.

33. PRO LC13/35, p. 52; LS 13/36, p. 54.

34. PRO Work 5/27, fo. 128.

35. Leslie G. Matthews, *The Royal Apothecaries* (London, 1967), pp. 104–7.

36. PRO LC5/138, p. 112.

37. PRO LC3/33.

38. *Pepys*, vol. II, p. 170.

39. WCA MSS. H441, H442.

40. Raymond Crawfurd, *The Last Days of Charles II* (Oxford, 1909), p. 26.

41. PRO Work 5/1, f. 121v; Work 5/3, fo. 110.

42. PRO Work 5/10, fo. 113.

43. PRO LC5/137, p. 98.

44. PRO Work 5/15, f. 117v.

45. *Pepys*, vol. VIII, p. 403.

46. *DNB*.

47. It is not absolutely certain that these rooms were at the Grainery; PRO LC5/12, p. 260; BL Lansdowne MS. 736, fo. 16.

48. PRO Work 5/15, fo. 25.

49. Colvin, *Dictionary*, p. 259; *HKW*, vol. V, pp. 31, 32, 471.

50. PRO Work 5/1, fo. 210; BL Lansdowne MS. 736, fo. 17.

51. N. Carlisle, *Gentlemen of the Privy Chamber* (London, 1829), p. 183; E. and J. Chamberlayne, *Angliae (Magnae Britanniae) Notitia; or the Present State of England (Great Britain)* (London, 1679), Pt. 3, p. 161; S. Wynne, 'The Mistresses of Charles II', Unpublished Ph.D., University of Cambridge, 1996, p. 261. I am grateful to Sonya Wynne for her help with this entry.

52. *DNB*.

53. BL Lansdowne MS. 736, fo. 11r.

54. PRO LC5/12, p. 231; PRO Work 5/13, fo. 57v.

55. PRO LC5/139, p. 368; PRO LC5/140, p. 89.

56. PRO LC5/140, p. 203.

57. PRO Work 5/25, f. 43; Work 5/26, f. 124v; Work 5/29, fo. 57; Work 5/35, f. 13v.

58. WCA MSS. H443, H444.

59. *HKW*, vol. V, p. 469; BL Lansdowne MS. 736, f. 17.

60. PRO LS13/252, p. 49.

61. PRO LC5/139, p. 368; LC5/140, p. 89.

62. PRO LC5/12, p. 205; LC5/138, p. 368.

63. PRO Work 5/1, f. 76.

64. PRO LC 5/137, pp. 410–11.

65. *Pepys*, vol. IV, p. 197.

66. PRO Work 5/9, ff. 160v, 170; Work 5/38, f. 72v.

67. PRO LC5/141 12 February 1676–7; LC5/142 25 October 1677.

68. *British Court*, p. 37

69. PRO Work 5/10, ff. 97, 150.

70. PRO Work 5/11, f. 38.

71. PRO Work 5/2, f. 143v.

72. WCA MS. F1114.

73. PRO LC5/138, pp. 281, 457.

74. WCA MS. H450.

75. BL Lansdowne MS. 736, f. 13v.

76. PRO LC5/137, p. 350.

77. PRO LC5/12, p. 299.

78. PRO Work 5/17, f. 111; Work 5/27, f. 120v; Work 5/29, f. 111.

79. PRO Work 5/43, f. 81.

80. J. Y. Akerman (ed.), 'Moneys Recieved and Paid for Secret Services of Charles II and James II', *Camden Society* (1851), p. 115.

81. PRO LS 13/8. Professor Robert Bucholz made this suggestion to me.

82. *ORH*, pp. 20–21.

83. PRO Work 5/27, f. 50.

84. S. Thurley, *Whitehall Palace* (Yale University Press, forthcoming).

85. PRO LS 13/252, p. 43; LS 13/253, p. 76.

86. PRO Work 5/30, f. 105; Work 5/33, f. 82; Work 5/19, f. 131.

52.

f. 10ᵛ.

L, vol. XVI, p. 205.

Work 5/32, f. 91.

Dom., 1664–5, p. 379.

Work 5/30, f. 74v.

, 112v.

08v; *Cal. SP. Dom., 1663–4*, p. 581.
of yorks bedchamber and mend-
& ye queens bedchamber', PRO

581; PRO Work 5/6, ff. 383–425v.
–425; Work 5/5, ff. 105, 119v, 129.
Work 5/15, f. 87.
PRO Work 5/9, ff. 424–55 and

9v, 98v, 109, 109v; Work 5/25, f. 53v.
73v, 74, 83v, 85v.
, 44, 95v; Works 5/36, 28v, 97v.
Work 5/25, f. 28; Work 5/29, f. 30.

, f. 7.

, PRO Work 5/35, f. 44.

, 150v.
–155v.

45v, 98; PRO Work 5/10, f. 127.
, f. 21.
lace: the King's and Queen's Apartments,
ng).
64, 65, 87v, 88v, 94v.

O Work 5/13, f. 105.

. 612.
, 328, 412–13; *SOL*, pp. 100–1,
and chronology differ; PRO Work

Cal. SP. Dom., 1666–7, p. 601.

, *op. cit.* (1674), p. 161.
Royal Ancient and Modern (London,

s necessaries for his majesty's use
o the Stuart Kings', *Costume*, No. 31

144 The date of George Kirke's Appointment PRO SP38/22, f. 20. The grant is misdated in the Calendar (*SP. Dom. 1663–4*, p. 45).
145 Maurice Ashley, *James II* (London, 1977), p. 95.
146 *SOL*, vol. XVI, pp. 82–5.
147 *SOL*, vol. XVI, pp. 18–19.
148 PRO Work 5/15, ff. 50v, 81.
149 O. Airy (ed.), 'The Lauderdale Papers 1639–1667', vol. 1, *Camden Society*, NS., XXXIV (1883–4), p. 157.
150 John G. Dunbar, 'The Building Activities of the Duke and Duchess of Lauderdale, 1670–82', *Archaeological Journal*, cxxxii, (1975), p. 228; PRO Work 5/145; LC5/141, p. 95.
151 Robert Bucholz suggested Thomas Lightfoot, Yeoman Huntsman of the Privy Buckhounds, PRO LC3/27, f. 37ᵛ. Sonya Wynne suggested Richard Lightfoot, Keeper of Bushy Park and Deputy Auditor and then Auditor of the Exchequer; *Cal. SP. Dom., 1667–8*, p. 153; *Cal. SP. Dom., 1669–72*, pp. 506, 581; J. C. Sainty, *Officers of the Exchequer* (List and Index Society special series, Vol. 18), p. 130. However I am inclined to agree with the suggestion of Robert Lightfoot made by Andrew Barclay; E. Chamberlayne, *op. cit.* (1682), p. 225; *ibid.* (1687), Pt. I, p. 227; *ibid.* (1692), Pt. I, p. 177; *ibid.* (1694), p. 268.
152 Leslie G. Matthews, *op. cit.*, p. 117.
153 *Cal. Treasury Books 1660–67*, p. 218; *Cal Treasury Books 1669–72*, p. 1341. I am grateful to Sonya Wynne for supplying me with these references.
154 PRO LC5/150, p. 240.
155 PRO Works 5/4, f. 146.
156 PRO LS 13/35, f. 26v; LS 13/254, f. 12ᵛ. I am grateful to Robert Bucholz for these references.
157 Anne Somerset, *Ladies in Waiting* (London, 1984), pp. 134–5.
158 PRO Work 5/9, f. 66; Work 5/10, f. 55; Work 5/11, f. 37.
159 BL Lansdowne MS. 736, f. 19ᵛ.
160 Colvin, *Dictionary*.
161 BL Lansdowne MS 736, f. 17ᵛ.
162 PRO LS13/9, f. 8A. Robert Bucholz points out that there were also Master Cooks for the Household Kitchen and the Queen's Kitchen. However this reference is most likely for the King's Privy Kitchen.
163 PRO LC5/137, p. 346.
164 BL Lansdowne MS. 736, f. 10ᵛ.
165 *HKW*, vol. III, p. 412; *HKW*, vol. v, pp. 3, 473.
166 BL Lansdowne MS. 736, f. 17ᵛ.
167 BL Lansdowne MS. 736, f. 17ᵛ.
168 Rupert Gunnis, *Dictionary of British Sculptors 1660–1851* (London, 1968), p. 254; Colvin, *Dictionary*, p. 539; *HKW*, vol. v, pp. 3–4, 471.
169 BL Lansdowne MS. 736, f. 17ᵛ.
170 *SOL*, vol. XIV, pp. 68–70; H. J. M. Green and S. J. Thurley, *op. cit.*, pp. 114–15.
171 PRO Work 5/4, f. 111.
172 *Pepys*, vol. IV, p. 371.
173 H. J. M. Green and S. J. Thurley, *op. cit.*, pp. 78–81.
174 PRO Work 5/4, ff. 440–481.
175 BL Harl MS. 1618, f. 224, 'charges for doing divers works in making lodgings in the old tennis court at Whitehall for ye Duke of Monmouth' (June 1664).
176 BL Add. MS. 15897, 'Goods plaised for the Duke and Duchess of Monmouth at thear Lodgings in ye Cockpitt, November ye 4th 1664'.
177 PRO Work 5/13, f. 154v.
178 PRO Work 5/23, f. 115.
179 PRO Work 5/23, ff. 423–434.
180 Mr Poyner, Mr Ross, Mrs Davis (where the linnen was kept), Mr Foord, Major Watson, Mr Cottle, Mr Shell.

[181] PRO Work 5/35, extraordinary account ff. 297–300.

[182] BL Lansdowne MS. 736, f. 13.

[183] PRO LC5/137, p. 1.

[184] J.Aubrey, *Brief Lives* (London, 1898), vol. II, p. 82.

[185] *Pepys*, vol. IX, pp. 415–16.

[186] *Pepys*, vol. VII, p. 410.

[187] *ORH*, pp. 36–7.

[188] Harl. MS. 6859. I am grateful to Anna Keay for pointing this out.

[189] BL Harl. MS. 1843, item 12.

[190] PRO LC5/138, p. 360.

[191] BL Lansdowne MS. 736, f. 11ᵛ; *SOL*, vol. XVI, p. 174.

[192] PRO Work 5/1, f. 141.

[193] *ORH*, pp. 16–17.

[194] PRO Work 5/1, f. 211.

[195] PRO Work 5/2, f. 87v; Work 5/27, ff. 93v, 112.

[196] PRO LC5/12, p. 210.

[197] PRO Work 5/23, f. 88v.

[198] WCA MSS. H446, F1101.

[199] PRO LC13/7, f. 13ᵛ. I am grateful to Robert Bucholz for identifying the Sergeant Porter for me.

[200] *Cal. SP. Dom., 1665–6*, pp. 42, 183; *Cal. SP. Dom., 1672–3*, p. 612.

[201] PRO LS13/253, p. 58; LS13/252, p. 175.

[202] PRO LS13/252, p. 261.

[203] PRO Work 5/15, ff. 66v, 79, 82, 93.

[204] BL Lansdowne MS 736, f. 13ᵛ.

[205] For instance PRO Work 5/29, f. 111; PRO LC5/12, p. 233.

[206] PRO LC5/138, p. 424.

[207] S. Thurley, *Whitehall Palace, op. cit.*

[208] *Ordinances*, p. 355.

[209] PRO LC5/140, p. 69.

[210] PRO Work 5/8, ff. 104, 107; Work 5/29, f. 19.

[211] PRO Work 5/11, f. 99v.

[212] PRO SP29/47, pp. 116–17.

[213] PRO Work 5/29, ff. 19, 21.

[214] PRO LC5/137, p. 303.

[215] PRO SP44/5, p. 135.

[216] *SOL*, vol. XIII, p. 244.

[217] PRO LC5/40, 5 September 1672; BL Lansdowne MS. 736, f. 5ᵛ.

[218] PRO LC5/137, p. 303; PRO Work 5/2, f. 159v; Work 5/3, f. 132.

[219] PRO Work 5/17, ff. 62v, 67v, 75.

[220] PRO LC5/140; PRO Work 5/21, ff. 29v, 394.

[221] Chamberlayne, *op. cit.* (1669).

[222] PRO LS13/7, f. 11ᵛ. I am grateful to Robert Bucholz for identifying these for me.

[223] PRO 5/48, f. 45.

[224] I am grateful to Sonya Wynne for identifying Lady Sayers for me. *Cal. SP. Dom., 1660–1*, p. 294; *Cal SP. Dom., 1667*, p. 493; *Cal. Treasury Books, 1667–8*, pp. 300, 641; Burke, *History of the Commoners* (London, 1836), vol. III, p. 505.

[225] PRO LC5/143, p. 414.

[226] *SOL*, vol. XIII, pp. 237n, 238.

[227] J. C. Sainty, *Office Holders in Modern Britain*, vol. II, 'Officials of the Secretaries of State 1660–1782' (University of London, 1973), pp. 56–7.

[228] I am grateful to Sonya Wynne for identifying Lady Silvius for me. S. Wynne, Ph.D., *op. cit.*, p. 261; *Cal. Treasury Books, 1667–8*, p. 598; *Cal. SP. Dom., 1670*, p. 437. Professor Bucholz pointed out Gabriel's post as Carver in Chamberlayne, *op. cit.* (1669).

[229] PRO LC5/138, p. 347; Work 5/10, ff. 67v, 80.

[230] PRO Work 5/9, ff. 67, 111.

[231] PRO Work 5/3, f. 88v.

[232] PRO LC5/12, f. 241.

[233] PRO Work 5/20 Extraordinary f. 296.

[234] PRO LC5/138, p. 370.

[235] *SOL*, vol. XVI, pp. 213–14.

[236] PRO Work 5/5, f. 59; Work 5/7, f. 18v; Work 5/9, f. 35; Work 5/15, f. 31; Work 5/29, f. 56v; Work 5/33, f. 27.

[237] PRO Work 5/15, f. 125.

[238] BL Lansdowne MS. 736, f. 17ᵛ.

[239] PRO Work 4/1.

[240] PRO Work 5/42 Extraordinary f. 297.

[241] J. C. Sainty, *Office Holders in Modern Britain*, vol. I, 'Treasury Officials 1660–1870' (University of London, 1972), p. 33.

[242] PRO Work 5/31, f. 133v; Work 5/35, f. 39.

[243] PRO Work 5/10, ff. 136v, 150; Work 5/32, f. 32a.

[244] PRO Work 5/9 Extraordinary, f. 459; Work 5/18 Extraordinary, f. 408.

[245] WCA MS. F1111.

[246] PRO Work 5/15, f. 56.

[247] PRO SP44/41, p. 47.

[248] PRO LC3/24, f. 12ᵛ; LC3/25, f. 37. I am grateful to Robert Bucholz for making this suggestion.

[249] PRO Work 5/10, f. 149.

[250] Anthony Richard Wagner, *The Records and Collections of the College of Arms* (Burke's Peerage, London, n.d.), p. 20.

[251] PRO LC5/86, pp. 1–27. Tom Campbell pointed out the existence of this inventory which he hopes to publish.

[252] *Wren Society*, vol. XVIII, pp. 18–19; C. L. Kingsford, *The Early History of Piccadilly, Liecester Square, Soho and Their Neighbourhood* (Cambridge, 1925), pp. 77, 120.

[253] PRO Work 5/3, ff. 69v, 139v.

[254] PRO LS13/252, p. 249.

[255] PRO LS 13/7, f. 12; LS13/252, f. 208. I am grateful to Robert Bucholz for these references.